W9-BNS-737

IT'S NOT ME, IT'S YOU!

IT'S NOT ME, IT'S YOU!

JON RICHARDSON

HarperCollins*Publishers*

HarperCollins*Publishers*
77–85 Fulham Palace Road,
Hammersmith, London W6 8JB

www.harpercollins.co.uk

First published by HarperCollins*Publishers* 2011

3

© Jon Richardson 2011

Guardian Weekend cover and 'Not Looking for Miss Immaculate with a
GSOH …' article by Jon Richardson © Guardian News + Media Ltd 2010

Jon Richardson asserts the moral right to be
identified as the author of this work

A catalogue record of this book is
available from the British Library

ISBN 978-0-00-741494-9

Printed and bound in Great Britain by
Clays Ltd, St Ives plc

All rights reserved. No part of this publication may be
reproduced, stored in a retrieval system, or transmitted,
in any form or by any means, electronic, mechanical,
photocopying, recording or otherwise, without the prior
written permission of the publishers.

MIX
Paper from
responsible sources
FSC® C007454

FSC is a non-profit international organisation established to promote the
responsible management of the world's forests. Products carrying the FSC
label are independently certified to assure consumers that they come
from forests that are managed to meet the social, economic and
ecological needs of present and future generations.

Find out more about HarperCollins and the environment at
www.harpercollins.co.uk/green

To do list

For all the friends and family members who tolerate my intolerance with inspiring grace

Perfectionism is the enemy of creation, as extreme self-solitude is the enemy of well-being.

John Updike

guardian weekend 13.02.10

I divorced my
husband...
...and married him
six weeks later

Jess Cartner-Morley
Fashion gets
minimalist

Impossible
perfectionist,
27, seeks
very
very
very
tidy
woman

INTRODUCTION

My name is Jon Richardson. I am an extreme perfectionist and I live on my own in the Wiltshire town of Swindon. I make my living as a stand-up comedian, travelling the country and talking about my life with what I intend to be hilarious consequences. In February 2010 I was asked by the *Guardian* newspaper's Weekend supplement to write an article on romance for their Valentine's Day special. I wrote the only article I felt able to write, namely my thoughts on the other side of the dating coin from the point of view of someone who is not in a relationship, has not been in one for some time, and feels more than a little trepidation at the thought of ever being in another one. Here is what I wrote and what was printed on 13 February.

NOT LOOKING FOR MISS IMMACULATE PERFECTION
WITH A GSOH ...

My last girlfriend was a loser. Literally. A wonderful and beautiful person, but prone to losing things: keys, money, credit cards, mobile phones. Each time she lost something, she would get upset and come to me for help and reassurance.

I, on the other hand, am a keeper. Not in the American sense that women throw themselves at me. Rather that if you were to ask me to lay my hands on a receipt for a pair of shoes I bought in 1997, I would be angry if it took me more than 90 seconds to locate it. Over to the filing cabinet I would stroll, R for Receipts, S for Shoes, and work through chronologically.

Had our relationship taken place in a sitcom, this juxtaposition would have led to hilarious consequences, as we laughed and joked about what a couple of cards we were and what kind of mixed-up world could ever have brought us together. Instead, we argued frequently over what she saw as something she was powerless to change, and I saw as a correctable weakness in her character.

In general I would say I find it difficult to accept other people's shortcomings. I am not an unfair person but I do think more effort is the solution to most problems. Not losing things is simply a matter of trying

harder to remember where you put them, isn't it? Popular music is no help here:

> If you love something,
> Let it go,
> If it comes back it's yours,
> That's how you kno-o-ow

Nonsense, Christina Aguilera! I say, 'If you love it, file it away under "Things I love". If it's required at a later date, you'll know exactly where it i-i-i-is.'

Wanting things my own way is not something I like about myself. From my love of right angles to my stubborn, black and white views on complex issues, I recognise I can be a very difficult person to be around. I also cannot fail to recognise many symptoms of obsessive-compulsive personality disorder. I have countless habits that I know serve no purpose but am powerless to avoid. I arrange my coins into ascending size in my pockets, for example, and nothing gives me more comfort than the knowledge that my forks, knives and spoons are all in the correct place, tessellating magnificently in their drawer.

I like to think that we're all on a scale where these tendencies are concerned. I am sure many people find it difficult to settle down to watch a DVD with a cobweb hanging behind the TV. But what if the cobweb isn't

behind the TV – or even in the same room – but lurking nauseatingly in the room next door? Could you still relax and enjoy the film? As a child I remember marvelling at how neatly my dad's sponge used to fit into the sponge-nook in his Ford Escort, but I don't know whether this was an early warning of who I would become or the reason for it.

If I were to have a catchphrase (and I like to think I don't), it would be, 'Fun must be sacrificed for efficiency.' It's harder to try all the time, it's harder to be monogamous than to sleep with whoever you want and it's harder to be disappointed by failure than it is to laugh and move on. That said, I have definitely crossed a line.

I no longer attempt new things because I am too afraid of failing. In my garage there exists a shrine to the person I promised I would become: scores of broken musical instruments, squash rackets and computers carefully boxed up to prevent them from hurting me any longer. I enjoy meals out, but limit my menu choices to things I've eaten before to reduce the risk of wasting money on a meal I don't enjoy.

For me there is no pleasure to be had in an experience unless I complete it perfectly first time. I'm not just talking about golf here, or bowling, but simply eating a biscuit, which can be done the right way or the wrong way in my world (depending obviously on the

4

biscuit in question). But there is another part of me that wonders why, if my way is so right, it has brought me to live alone, far from family and friends, in Swindon.

Swindon, which is somewhere between Bristol and London, is a town that is synonymous with comedy, not that anything famously funny has happened here, but people seem to laugh when you say that you live in Swindon. Like Slough, it simply inspires the pity that is such a constituent part of British humour. 'His life is clearly shit, this is going to be brilliant!'

I moved here when I dropped out of university, stepped off the treadmill and took control of my future. I wanted somewhere I could be anonymous, where there was nothing to distract me from what I wanted to achieve. Unless I developed a sudden fascination with roundabouts, Swindon seemed the perfect place to reinvent myself. At no point in my teens did I think, 'I can only hope that by my late twenties I will have my own place, close to a big Asda and with equally handy transport links to Cirencester or Wootton Bassett.' Yet here I am.

I should point out here that there are many positives to be had from taking life as seriously as I do. For example, I don't remember the last time I fell over. Even in the recent snow and ice I stayed upright, although less by stealthy catlike grace than by steadfastly refusing to leave my house. I would rather stay at home than take

a tumble on my way to Morrisons and be laughed at by passers-by. Falling is a good example of something that can be seen in one of two ways: either it is an unavoidable consequence of our get-up-and-go lifestyles, or it is an inability to perform such a rudimentary task that it cannot be tolerated. Needless to say, I subscribe to the latter ideology.

When it comes to the simple pleasures in life, half an hour with a glass of beer and an episode of *You've Been Framed!* is hard to beat. Occasionally I have to rewind and watch the same clip over and over again (I'm talking about you, girl falling into boating lake). I laugh uncontrollably but it's not the suffering of another human being I enjoy, it's the relief. 'It could have been me!' I think, as I watch pensioners grappling unsuccessfully with pogo sticks and dogs running into glass doors. I treat each show as a training manual for life, crossing off pastimes that represent an unnecessary risk: flying remote-controlled aircraft in misty fields, spinning round in the garden with an upturned rake on my chin, carrying a carefully iced birthday cake. Falls end in pain and humiliation; falling over, falling from grace. Even, in my experience, falling in love.

My last relationship ended in 2003 (it seems the final thing my girlfriend lost was her desire to put up with my constant nitpicking) and I decided to take a break for a while. There is no reason, I thought, why people can't be completely happy on their own. Initially I revelled in returning home to find that everything was exactly where I had left it; that there was as much milk as there had been when I last used some and that I could watch whatever I wanted on TV. The novelty has now definitely worn off and the grass on the other side of the fence is a sickly, HD green.

I haven't woken up with a cup of tea by the bed for seven years. It seems such a small thing (and those of you reading this who are in relationships will probably be thinking that at least when you make a cup of tea yourself it doesn't taste like crap) but it's one of a thousand things I miss about having someone around to take care of you. I have spent my entire adult life getting things the way I want them and all I want now is someone to give it all up for.

When you look into the eyes of the person you love, it is easy to forget that there is anything else in the world besides the river of emotion flowing between you. Why, then, do you want to push them out of the window five minutes later for putting a wet teaspoon into the sugar? Have they not been told a thousand times that the sight of the brown clusters this forms makes you feel sick? Of course they have ... so they must be doing it because they hate you! You hate them, too. How could you have been so blind earlier? Then, as you are getting up to charge headlong in their direction,

7

they laugh – and you remember why you love them – and the whole exhausting cycle begins anew.

But if true love is hard, then one-night stands hold little appeal for a perfectionist like myself. In my head I have a carefully ranked list, with things I do well at the top, and things I do badly at the bottom. About two-thirds of the way down, between making trifle and rewiring a plug, is 'showing a woman the night of her life between the sheets'. I would no sooner go clubbing and pick up a woman for sex than I would run on to the pitch at Old Trafford and start showing off my keepy-uppy skills.

My friends can't believe how long I have gone without having sex. I see it rather like going to the cinema: of course it's fun and if we all had our own way we would do it as often as possible, but if we don't get round to going, it's probably just because there were far more important things to do.

In the last few years I have met women who have made me think that it might be time to end my self-imposed isolation. From those whom I have been out with a few times, to strangers who have walked past me on a train, a brief encounter will set my mind racing about what the future could be like for us and remind me of all the things I currently miss out on. Believe me, holidays abroad, lazy Sundays and trips to Monkey Forest are all much less fun alone.

INTRODUCTION

Things never get far before I find some reason to knock down the idealised vision I have created. If they are attractive, I wonder whether I am being superficial. If they are funny, I wonder whether they are funnier than me. Perhaps they will call or text too frequently and I will feel harassed, or they won't text or call at all and I will become convinced they despise me. It could be something as small as a 'Hope your OK' text, which will send me spiralling into apocalyptic visions of a life without apostrophes or question marks.

On the other hand, do I want someone like myself? An equally quarrelsome perfectionist, only with breasts and less body hair? Absolutely not, it would drive me insane. According to the American author and philosopher Sam Keen, 'We come to love not by finding the perfect person, but by seeing an imperfect person perfectly.'

Great, you would think, I can finally stop looking for Mr or Miss Right and just work on convincing myself that Mr or Miss Not Bad But Smells Funny And Has An Oddly Small Mouth is actually perfect.

This is far more difficult than it sounds.

In the early stages of a relationship, what I call 'the lying stage', two people will display only that side of their character that is attractive to a prospective partner. 'You love Dostoevsky, too? Wow! Well, aren't we just two peas in a long-winded, Russian pod?'

A bond will subsequently form based upon the fictitious life that these two invented personalities could share. Friends and family will be informed that the search for 'the one' is off. We can all get to this point easily enough, but the real challenge comes as the stresses of compromise become too much and the real person begins to manifest itself.

He wants to wash up as they cook, before residue has a chance to dry out and stick, whereas she wants to leave it to soak and do it after *The Simpsons*. She wants to go on holiday to a place where they can do and see things of interest; he wants to go somewhere he can drink by a pool. She wants to paint the bedroom red and he wants to get SkyPlus. She wants to have a baby and he still wants to get SkyPlus.

In comedy cliché terms, this is known as the point when two people finally feel comfortable enough to break wind in one another's company. Curiously, this is seen as a good thing. For me, it signals the beginning of the end. From the peak of potential perfection you descend down through 'going to the toilet with the door open', past 'perfunctory sex' and into 'cold, dead stares across the breakfast table'. I could quite happily get through a 40-year marriage without ever suspecting that my partner went to the toilet at all.

As I read this back to myself (the last line especially), my conclusion is, 'Wow. That guy really needs a

girlfriend!' Surely no relationship could be as difficult as living with my own perfectionism? If I met the woman of my dreams, would I mind her organising our CDs by genre and not alphabetically? Could I let her keep the knives to the left of the forks in our shared cutlery drawer? Of course, I'm not a fool. But that's not what is really being surrendered in a relationship. What you give to someone, when you give him or her your heart, is control over your happiness. Their moods and reactions can dictate absolutely whether you skip out of bed in the morning or are afraid to go home after work. There is no middle ground; the joy is in the surrender.

I know that no one is happy all the time, but I have learned that unhappiness can be an awful lot easier to deal with if you know you are responsible for it, and therefore responsible for changing it. It's in my nature to focus on the negative details so that they can be fixed. The problem is that I sometimes forget to enjoy life in the meantime and just go looking for the next thing to improve upon. As much as I want that cup of tea in the morning, and all that goes with it (security and a sense of contentment, not just sugar and some toast), I am scared that my desire to make someone perfectly happy would be an impossible pursuit and the cause of much unhappiness.

I can't shake off my feeling that the only inevitable result of a long-term relationship is that you will see

somebody else's weaknesses and they will see yours. Eventually you will lose respect for one another and either break up or find yourselves locked into a love-less future. Am I right? Of course not! Can I change? I sincerely hope so because, as it stands, it is clearly me who is the loser, desperately looking for a keeper.

★   ★   ★

Friends warned me against being so honest in my writing, but since my life is not one of tremendous interest or victory over incredible hardship, honesty is just about all I have to offer. Too much detail not withstanding, the response to the article was fantastic and I received a number of letters and emails from people who had read it and wanted to tell me that they felt the same way as I did and suffered similarly with a desire not to be alone, unfortunately coupled with an intolerance of others. I also received a number of very kind, somewhat romantic offers from women who told me that they would be happy to step into the breach, as it were, and end my relationship drought. It would have been cynical of me to say the least to have written an article with the sole intention of using it to secure sexual conquests and, if anything, I felt almost annoyed that anyone reading the article would misinterpret my tale of being trapped in my solitude as a call to my arms. Through the various responses I gained

confidence in the knowledge that I was not alone in what I was feeling and was pleased to note that I may have helped others who feel the same way. It seems the world is full of people who do not, in spite of what we see in sitcom and in film, go on multiple dates with people they meet in bars and coffee shops and who do not seem to know exactly what it is they are looking for, let alone how and where to find it. I therefore decided to write in more detail about what I see as the truth about relationships and how my brain works, and the result of that work is the book you hold in your hands.

If you are reading these words then let me thank you for not only finding the book but also making room for it in your life. I am loathe to spend too much time so early in our relationship telling you what you are *not* about to read, since that game could easily go on for ever, but there are a couple of things I would like to point out at the outset.

The first thing is that this book is not an autobiography. I make no apologies for the fact that I will not be writing about where I went to school, who my best friend was when I was five years old or when I first ate a kumquat (though the omission of the latter owes more to the fact that I'm still not entirely sure what a kumquat is, much less whether or not I have ingested one).

Where a childhood memory helps explain something of how I became the man I am today, it has been
included, but this is not the tale of how a child from the
cold wastelands of t'north of t'England worked his way
up the ladder from being the guy in the kitchen who
puts the little salads on the side of baguettes to fulfill-
ing his dream of becoming a full-time stand-up comic.
That is not a story I intend to write until I am sat at a
scruffy old desk in a battered little potting shed somewhere in the Lake District with a dog curled up at my
feet, confident that the most interesting parts of my life
have been lived and any of the people I might upset or
insult are not around any more. The year of publication
of this book will be my twenty-eighth on the planet, so
I do not consider for one second that I have had a *bio*
worth *graphing* about, *auto*matically or otherwise.

Rather than being a chronological journey across my
years, it is the tale of another journey – the most important journey on which I find myself – my quest for
perfection. Perfection is what drives me in everything
I do; be it finding the perfect partner, living the perfect
day or simply constructing and consuming the perfect
sandwich.

When speaking of the perfect day, people tend to
imagine one spectacular event, the beauty of which
overshadows any minor shortcoming which might
have occurred up to that point – walking along a beach

at sunset, drinking red wine on a shagpile rug by the glowing embers of a fire in a French chateau or, for a lucky few, making love at dawn on the top of Mount Everest. As special as those individual events may be, that's not what I'm talking about at all; that's not how perfect days work in my book. The perfect day is not a once-in-a-lifetime occurrence, it is something that can happen every day if you're willing to put in the effort. A perfect day exists independently from the tasks that need to be completed on that day and concerns only how efficiently they have been carried out. It begins well before the perfect cup of tea, it starts the moment you open your eyes – or, for the real hardcore, the moment you finish your 'To Do' list the night before, rewriting if necessary to eliminate spelling mistakes and ensure even word spacing and neat handwriting. So fragile is it, that it can be undone by so little as a stubbed toe or an odd sock. A perfect day is one without mistakes and they are to be utterly cherished.

I do not subscribe to the view that mistakes are a part of life; they are not. This is not to say that more cannot be learned from a mistake than anything else; that *is* true, but that is not an excuse for making them. Mistakes are caused, in the main, by a failure to plan properly, try hard enough or pay enough attention to detail. If you are willing to take personal responsibility for each failure, however small, then you can strive to

eliminate errors altogether. I am of the belief that the 'point of life' is not a question, but a noun; an actual point-scoring system that rewards perfect execution of a task on a measurable scale:

* Made someone smile? **Gain two life points.**
* Made someone cry? **Lose five life points.**
* Dropped a spoon? **Lose one life point.**
* Cheated on your wife and children by sleeping with the ex-partner of an ex-teammate because you are a multi-millionaire Premier League footballer and you are arrogant enough to think you can get away with anything? **Lose a million life points.**

And so on.

It gives me satisfaction to think that not only is there such a thing as right and wrong in this world, but there is a way of measuring exactly how right and wrong something might be. People would like to think that the decisions we make in our lives are ephemeral and impossible to quantify but they aren't really. Most of the things we do that will hurt other people are known to us before we carry them out, and rather than discover afterwards that there were hidden consequences to our actions, in truth we simply make a value judgement on whether or not what we stand to gain by upsetting someone else justifies the decision for ourselves.

16

The ultimate goal of my point-scoring system is, of course, to allow someone to become the Ultimate Human on Earth. I do not believe in a god, but I would like to think somebody somewhere is keeping score for us. New players are constantly being added to the worldwide league, international transfers are being made each and every day, regardless of whether the window is open or closed and, as is always the case in life as well as sport, the up-and-coming talent seems to lack some of the grit and honesty of the generation that came before it.

After each day's play I go to bed at night, acutely aware of whether or not I won the day, took a battering away from home or whether the world and I ground out a well-fought draw. The commentator in my head goes on trotting out his clichés like sheep jumping over a fence to send me off to sleep, or keeping me awake if further match analysis is needed.

Whatever the benefits of living my life this way – and I hope that as you read on you will discover that there are many – it is not an instant recipe for happiness. I am definitely guilty of spending so much of my time trying to do things in what I deem to be the correct manner that I can sometimes forget entirely to enjoy them. While some people may eat a biscuit in a certain idio-syncratic way for fun, I do it because I believe it to be the correct way of doing so and deviation constitutes

failure. I don't need to tell you which the best part of a Jaffa Cake or a Jammy Dodger is, do I? Why create another disappointing memory by leaving yourself with the worst bit at the end?

It is a source of some frustration for me that Cadbury's have been collecting data on the many ways people choose to eat their Creme Eggs for years now and yet stubbornly refuse to publish their results. We need to take public ownership of the company and force them to release their facts and figures so that we can find out once and for all what the correct answer is, for there must be one. What if I have been doing it wrong all this time?

My weirdness aside, if I am to find any friends, particularly a girlfriend, she will almost certainly have to be a human. My previous track record tends to suggest that of all the species that exist on the planet, it has so far been exclusively humans to whom I find myself sexually attracted. This is a good thing legally if nothing else.

The unfortunate coincidence is that humans are also top of my list of creatures I would most like to see wiped off the face of the planet. Sometimes cats are well placed just behind them, and wasps certainly never manage to get out of the danger zone, but neither of

these last two can be reasoned with and so are equally worthy of my fear, but not so much of my hatred. I fear all that which cannot be talked out of causing harm – drunks and children also fall into this category.

Most animals that do harm have not evolved a thought process capable of rationalising their actions or else they only act in self-defence. Humans, on the other hand, have conscious thought and therefore their malicious acts score double points. I do not subscribe to the view that we have been placed here by some kind of higher being; I do not believe we are special enough to warrant that kind of attention. We are simply a thing, that lives in a place, and one day something will happen to that place (either because of us or in spite of us, some kind of cosmic event beyond our comprehension let alone ability to influence) and we won't be here any more. Our gods will go with us when we leave.

If I might submit my entry here for the award for most turgid and illogical metaphor in literature: In the giant nightclub that is the universe, the clock will sooner or later reach ten-to-two and the bouncers of time will pick us up off the ground and fling us through the doors of existence onto the pavement of history, and we will be missed no more than a tapeworm is missed by its host.

The world will move on regardless and then in millions of years something else will live here and

perhaps it will dig us up from the ground and marvel at how small our brains were and try to piece together the story of how we moved and where we lived and how we died. But maybe they won't. That's what I believe anyway, but for a man who can barely get through the day without losing his temper at something so small as to be invisible to most people – as you will discover later – perhaps speculating on such spiritual matters is a waste of time.

Whatever the chain of events that has put us, in our current form, on this planet at this time, I feel far more privileged to exist when I consider the millions of years of evolution and cosmic shift that has made our lives possible than by the thought that we were manufactured, and our world made for us, by a man in the sky.

Life created by a supreme being is but a toy, a plaything for levels of existence far beyond our own, but life that exists on a knife edge, life that is a gift from our many ancestors who braved their surroundings and adapted so that we might one day master them – that is a gift to be cherished.

The person sat opposite you on the bus is not much more than a mayfly in the great scheme of things, given a brief window in the eternity of time to live and to love, to taste strawberries and to ride bicycles and experience cold sores and stomach upsets, to have baths that had too much cold water in them and to hate the taste of oysters and not understand poetry. There is so much for each of us to get done and so little time to do it in that we can't possibly do it without help, so we should make space for one another, clear a path to allow those of us through who need a helping hand.

A smile at a stranger on the bus can be all it takes to propel someone who is tired a little further onward on a grey day, or perhaps just start by moving your bag off that seat next to you so that the old lady can sit down?

Oh you won't? I see. Did you pay for two seats? No.

You just like to have two seats to yourself? OK.

But the evolution thing? They all worked so hard to get us here and you could just …?

I see, you've had a bad day at work and you …? Right.

Well then, fuck all mankind, may we all disappear in a great flash of light and let cats and dogs rule the planet for a while and see if they can behave any less ignorantly than we do – we with our evolved thinking and deep beliefs. People who see my shows have sometimes described my thoughts as a stream of consciousness, but I think a river of scorn would be more like it. I don't mean to hate people, I get forced into it.

As you can see it takes very little for the good man in me, the one who wants to care and to believe the best of people, to be suffocated. Let me witness the success of a moral person any day of the week over the success

of a twat – show me an England football team filled with players who give their money to charity and congratulate their opponents and I will applaud their ten–nil defeat in a way I could never applaud a narrow one–nil victory by a bunch of greedy, philandering morons. Struggle to do something right and I will help you; profit in selfishness and I will hope you die. There's the line, right there.

ODD COMIC'S DEFINITION

In talking about some of the things I obsess about and my routines for executing certain tasks, a certain level of compulsion will become apparent. While I may appear to display certain traits of Obsessive Compulsive Disorder, I am keen to point out from the outset that I do not refer to myself as a sufferer. I have never been given, nor sought, a medical diagnosis for my mental condition, but rather consider myself to be someone who has been allowed to develop certain habits, and beyond that has been able to exploit those habits for comedic effect. I do not seek to make light of an illness that can cripple lives and leave people unable to function in modern society and the over-simplistic treatment of OCD for comedy is a huge bugbear of mine.

I know I have countless habits that serve no purpose but I am powerless to avoid them, and it is true that I

am frequently frustrated by a number of things that I should let go of (currently the fact that the spine of the foreign DVD I have ordered has text running in the opposite direction to all the others on the shelf, making it impossible to file it neatly). But I am constantly annoyed when I hear jokes that portray all sufferers of OCD as nothing more than glove-wearing weirdos who cannot leave a room without switching the lights on and off three times. Anyone who regularly attends live stand-up comedy will know this as 'The Rain Man Effect', whereby a comparison to the famous Dustin Hoffman film role is enough to explain away any odd quirk of behaviour and elicit gales of laughter from a room full of drunks.

Aside from my annoyance at the confusion of different conditions this represents, I believe compulsion, much like sexuality or preference for olives, is a question of sliding scale, where there are not simply sufferers or non-sufferers but degrees of suffering. There are those among us who are unable to stop washing their hands from one minute to the next and there are those who can go for weeks without washing their hands or wondering what makes up the rainbow of dirt underneath their fingernails, but there are far more people somewhere in the middle who wash their hands when appropriate and shudder slightly when they push the toilet door on exit and find that it is wet.

Similarly, I do not claim to be a hypochondriac, but nor can I deny that I haven't on occasion lain awake at night fretting that the red mark on my arm is a hideous tropical disease picked up from the unwashed grapes in my fruit salad rather than the truth, the result of a drunken fall. But as I am keen to stress, the compulsion is but a facet of my perfectionism, an attribute far more associated with Obsessive Compulsive Personality Disorder than OCD.

To give you an idea, this is the kind of self-deluding perfectionist I am: Leeds United fans of the early 1990s will be familiar with the chant 'There's only one Gary Speed.' This would seem to be a valid enough point, except for the fact that in my 1994 Merlin sticker album there isn't – there are two. One is where he should be, by his own name, but another one is obscuring the empty pane that represents the Brian Deane I never found. I couldn't bear having failed to complete my album, so safe in the knowledge that anyone simply skimming through to check for gaps would not notice my deception I duplicated my Garys. I hereby apologise fully to all teenage sticker collectors for invalidating the joy of an honest completion, to all the staff at Merlin and mostly to my friend Lee, whom I told I had finished my sticker book simply because I was jealous that he had finished his … or had he really? I have my doubts!

INTRODUCTION

The guilt I feel is genuine, but in truth it is not so much guilt at having deceived my friends, but a still burning ember of disappointment deep in my soul at my failure to complete the book honestly. Yes, I take my life *that* seriously. My fear of failure is so extreme that even when on my own I find it difficult to accept mistakes. Like most men who live alone, there are telltale signs in my décor and furniture that I am a bachelor. There is, for example, no settee in my living room. I experimented with one for a while, but found that with space relatively tight in a living-room/diner, the room taken up by the extra seat simply could not be justified when weighed up against the number of visitors I receive. It was duly replaced by a leather reclining massage chair and, with some rejigging, the extra space was put to good use and allowed for the purchase of a much bigger television and a drinks table.

The most obvious sign of my singledom is probably the dartboard which hangs on the back of the door (or when the dartboard is put away behind the table, the thousands of tiny dart holes covering the door, but for a small circle in the upper middle). There is something in the rhythmic back and forth of darts, the clearly defined boundaries and the rewards it offers for accuracy and repetition that I enjoy. My favourite pub game is, of course, snooker. Any game whose rules basically amount to finding a table covered in mess and slowly

and methodically putting it all away out of sight is one with which I can empathise emphatically.

As much as I enjoy darts, I must confess to not being very good at it, hence the holes in the door. And the door frame. And even the skirting board. The reason I am not very good at darts, and the reason I am not very good at many things, is my stubborn refusal to accept my shortcomings. Each time I throw a dart and miss my intended target, instead of trying to work out what went wrong and correct my technique for long-term success, I get so pissed off with myself that the next two darts are bound to be even wider off the mark than the first.

Professional players have reacted with greater calm and maturity to missing vital darts in World Championship finals than I have on my own at 2am on a wet Tuesday night in my shitty little flat. It won't be long before the dartboard annoys me so much that I react as any true man might when threatened – by breaking it and hiding it in the garage. In my garage exists a shrine to the person I promised I would become; a man who can paint great works of art, play squash to international standards, and write and compose his own guitar concertos. The history of his heartache is etched across a landscape of broken-stringed racquets and half-painted canvases with the word 'BASTARD' drunkenly scrawled across them in black paint.

INTRODUCTION

I cannot bear to be bad at things I love. I long to play the piano but the sound I make with my clumsy fingers crashing down irregularly on the keys is enough to shatter my spine. Like loving someone so much that all you can bear to do is strangle them to death for fear that they might not love you back, I can never go near a brand new piano in case of what might happen.

I hope that in these pages there will be some counsel for anyone who has ever lost their temper at an inanimate object, for those lost sheep who have sacrificed whole afternoons calling a biro a shiteater because it ran out part way through an important document. It is not the pen that is to blame, of course, but the entire cosmos that has decided to make you its victim for that day – but you can't very well snap the cosmos in half and jump all over it can you? That is a much longer game.

RICHARDSON'S LAW OF MOMENTS

There will, of course, be a small number of people reading this who will not be able to associate *at all* with the desire to do things in a certain way time after time. If you think you fall into that category, then you should be made aware of this fact: I probably wouldn't click with you if we met. I doubt it bothers you, since by nature you are probably an impulsive person who

doesn't carry with them the rejections of the past, preferring instead to 'live for the moment'. Well, let me tell you that you can keep your moments; I for one do not like the present.

People who tell you that they live their lives *in the moment* are, in my experience, only doing so because they are afraid of their future or ashamed of their past. These are people for whom thinking of anything other than the fork in their hand or the song in their head or the next step they are going to take frightens them so much that they pretend it is some kind of inspiring and advisable philosophy to do simply whatever it occurs to them to do at that moment in time.

Not only does this life philosophy appal me, I am also annoyed by the fact that it is me who is preached at for having forgotten what it is to be truly alive. Optimists and thrill seekers are riddled with sickeningly sweet sayings and mottos that serve to reinforce their flawed beliefs. People who style their hair for hours to make it look as though it hasn't been styled at all will send you emails with pictures of cats doing water sports and taglines like 'Yesterday is history, tomorrow is a mystery. Today is a gift, that's why they call it the present.'

The problem with simplistic and poetic sentiments such as these is that they sound so nice and catchy. I can understand completely why people choose to

think that way, of course. Who doesn't want to believe that every day of their life is a perfectly wrapped gift from the hands of fate? Well, it isn't, not as far as I am concerned. There are no easily quotable sayings about just knuckling down and getting on with life in all its inconsistent and unfair glory, and if there were, they wouldn't rhyme or have witty wordplays so people would choose to ignore them. There is simply too much to be done for us all to go around 'enjoying ourselves'. When the world is perfect, then we can all sit down and eat jelly beans, but for now the fact that things are going well for you just means that you are in a position to alleviate someone else's suffering for a while.

Not living in the present doesn't mean not enjoying life at all – far from it! Things can be enjoyed all the more when you appreciate the sacrifice and hard work that went into their organisation, like a slow-cooked piece of meat. All the gristle and toughness that were there at the beginning have been worn away through consistent application of heat over time to leave behind something as smooth as silk. Brace yourselves for plenty more unjustifiable food similes. When you plan your life properly every day can be as exciting as Christmas Eve and you never have to suffer the comedown that is Boxing Day. Just look at Boxing Day as the eve of the eve (and so on) of Christmas Eve.

I seem to be at a time of life where my thoughts are involuntarily turning towards more permanent things, relationships that will last and where I want to be when I settle down, but I also know that I'm still at an age when I should be enjoying my freedom and taking risks and making mistakes.

Apparently 'making mistakes' is what your youth is for and, whilst I can't say I agree, I will certainly concede that life was a lot simpler when I wasn't expected at all to be thinking long term and living from day-to-day was simply how it was. I am no longer sure that I am a better balanced person with a greater understanding of myself for having spent the last ten years taking life so seriously. Perhaps I should have spent more of my time in nightclubs, having promiscuous sex with people I never intended to see again? It just never appealed to me.

The last time I went back to a girl's house for an impromptu house party I spent most of the night straightening out rugs, putting down coasters and alphabetising DVDs while all around me people got off with whoever was closest and gradually headed off to various rooms to make more mess, no doubt. I ended up getting violently drunk, tutting at a number of strangers and walking home. I only just about made it.

Personally I alphabetise my DVD collection, but like most of the things I do I maintain that this is nothing to do with OCD, this is simply common sense. How can

you expect to find the film you are looking for if you do not have a system in place on the shelf? Given that the likely piece of information you have about what you want to watch is its title, it is logical to sort them thus.

Obviously if you are the kind of person who thinks, 'I'm not sure what I want to watch but I want it to have been directed by John Hughes', then you may sort by director, but who does that? The alphabetised system is one that is easy to identify so there is no excuse for replacing a DVD wrongly and yet people do it simply to annoy me. If I have guests, rare though the occasion may be, after each trip to the toilet or into the kitchen I will return to a room filled with sniggering guests staring at me intently.

'We've moved something!'

And the gales of laughter continue as I move around looking for the swapped DVDs or the rotated ornament, like Annie Wilkes in *Misery*. Perhaps the reason I don't have guests more often is the gleeful way in which they try to make me feel uncomfortable in my own home, or perhaps they move things as a way of making themselves feel more comfortable. Such a sanitised environment cannot be easy to relax in, so perhaps they are trying to make themselves feel at home, which I suppose is valid. I myself resent being asked to remove my shoes when entering a friend's house, even though I understand the reasoning behind it. It nevertheless

sets a precedent for a visit which must leave behind no reminder. When you leave, I don't even want to know you were ever here.

Must I really make a mess to make people feel comfortable in my house? How far do we go in making ourselves appear weak to elevate those around us? This willingness not only to expose weaknesses but to revel in them is what has led to the misguided belief that breaking wind in front of your partner is some kind of display of trust.

'I love you so much I want you to see all sides of me, inside and out.'

I have argued with several people who believe that breaking wind is a part of life and therefore should not be hidden from someone you care about once you are over the initial dating period in which the desire to impress is paramount.

I am of the opinion that there is never a point in a relationship at which it stops being a lack of respect for someone near to you to force them to inhale the smell of your own semi-digested gut slurry. Even writing these words makes me feel uncomfortable and you can call it anal retention or weirdness if you like but if you truly can't be bothered to leave the room to break wind then you are on a slippery slope which ends with you leaving the toilet door open and continuing a conversation with your partner while you void your bowels.

Such is my desire only to see the best parts of my partner and vice-versa that I must confess to being able to remember each time I have seen someone I was in love with fall over. I cannot help but be disappointed by such a shocking inability to perform such a simple task as staying upright. I can't remember the last time I fell over, mostly because if it does happen it is through drunkenness which gladly takes my ability to remember anything at all away with my dexterity, but I place my feet very carefully to avoid the possibility. If we learn to walk as toddlers how can it be that, once we have mastered the basics, we accept that we don't get any better at it? As a fully grown adult I expect at very least that I will be able to stay upright in polite society at all times.

LOOKING FOR MS VERY VERY VERY TIDY

I hope this book won't be a predictable journey: I'm no rule-following loser all the time! I even took my dinner out of the microwave last night barely thirty seconds into the required one minute resting time. That's right, I'm bad too, when I need to be and when I have properly assessed the potential risk. Deal with it. A few small indiscretions aside, I'm not unaware that my life isn't following the patterns for someone my age. Even I catch myself doing things that I would be embarrassed

for anyone else to find out about. In the spirit of full disclosure, here is a list.

* **I find myself washing up at eleven p.m. on a Saturday night**
Nothing makes me feel more like a loser than seeing myself reflected in the kitchen window wearing marigolds and scrubbing at soufflé moulds on what is widely accepted to be 'party night'. I wouldn't want to be out at a club, and I don't want to wake up on Sunday morning with a load of dirty dishes staring me down while I make a cup of tea, but still I am aware of how my situation looks and cannot help but feel as though in the eyes of my peers I ought to be ashamed, which isn't much worse than actually being ashamed.

* **I smile more at dogs than their owners**
I have rarely met a dog I didn't like. Little fat dumpy ones, who look like grumpy old men as they waddle down the street; big, tall hairy ones, who look as though they are trying to convince you that they are really too cool to be tied up outside Wilkinson's; bright-eyed, bouncy, energetic ones, who make no effort to disguise the fact that every second of their life is a

revelation to them, they want to meet everyone, to smell everything and to run as fast as possible at all times. I wish I felt the same.

* **I laugh at jokes the Eggheads make**
I watch this teatime quiz without exception while I have my first glass of wine on days when I do not have to work. My favourite kind of people to watch on television are those who give off the impression that no matter how much they do, they will never quite be any good at it. Nervous, embarrassed by their immense founts of knowledge, the Eggheads are the ringleaders of this club. You'd be more likely to find them sharing a packet of pork scratchings at your local real-ale pub than on the red carpet at a movie premiere, and that's suits me just fine.

* **I cut recipes out of magazines (and bake them)**
Weekend magazines are filled with what are, in reality, middle-class lifestyle pornographic photographs rather than recipes. It's not that any of us really believe that we will one day spend our weekends making oxtail soup from scratch and serving it in hearty bowls on wooden boards with home-made bread fresh from the Aga, but for the two hours we spend leafing through

35

someone's discarded pull-out supplements in the pub on a Sunday afternoon. I do; I have to hold on to the dream.

* **Wearing an apron**
  Not even a novelty apron, at that. Middle-aged husbands tending to barbecues in the summer can wear novelty aprons – that is all.

Whether you are a lot like me, a more extreme version of me, or scarcely recognisable as the same species as me, I hope that you will discover in yourself something of the obsessive. I truly do think we all have something deep down inside us that annoys us irrationally and that this sometimes unexplainable response is part of what makes us human.

Perhaps without thinking, you will take a toilet roll off its holder when visiting a friend's house, and replace it the other way around to ensure that the roll unravels forwards rather than down the back against the wall. Perhaps you subconsciously clean the rim of your wine glass with your napkin in a restaurant or have an overwhelming urge to straighten paintings that rest crooked. The part of you that makes your legs tingle with the urge to get up and correct a poorly hanged piece of art is the same as the part of me that makes me keeps all the items on my desk parallel with one another. It is a belief in the right way of things even if you cannot always explain why it seems so right.

Some authors travel through time with their readers, others take them to far off shores. In the quest on which you are about to accompany me – to find my Significantly Tidy Other – I will basically lock you in an enclosed space with a lunatic.

Large, deep, metaphysical questions will come bubbling up to the surface, like why, if my execution of everything has been so perfect, have I not been in a relationship for such a long time? Is the problem really with everyone else, or is there something wrong with me? Is there someone out there who could make all this better, and if I found them would I ruin it by expecting too much of them?

I suppose the ultimate question I am asking is: who is responsible for our own happiness, is it ourselves, or the person we are constantly looking for? Is my happiness really down to me ... Or is it you?

It is probably worth asking at this point, who exactly is my perfect woman? Attractive? Yes. Intelligent. Of course. Blah blah blah ... All of these things together? Absolutely not! What on earth would a woman like that be doing with a man such as myself? Cheating on him, that's what.

Just the thought of this makes me feel stressed and uncomfortable, and whenever I feel stressed and

uncomfortable, there is only one remedy: I have to sit down and write a 'To do' list. So I turn to tomorrow's date and start scheduling …

SATURDAY

11.39

CLOSE EVERY DOOR

I definitely remember dropping a bin bag half filled with rubbish into my wheelie bin on the way to my car. I remember putting my suitcase in the boot, beside my emergency box and climbing into the driver's seat. I turned the key in the ignition – I remember that because the radio came on and they were talking about rap music so I turned it straight off – and then I pulled out of my driveway and on to the road. After driving about two hundred metres I signalled left – though nobody was behind me – and pulled over to the side of the road, stopped and applied my handbrake. This is where I have been for around three minutes now. It has started.

Did you lock the door?

The trouble is that while I'm thinking about whether I locked the door, I'm also thinking about Gemma.

I cannot stop thinking about her, which is a problem. I am certain that she would absolutely hate it if she knew what I was doing now and I do not want her to end up hating me. I just don't know how you explain this kind of thing to someone who could never understand living this way.

It is an unfortunate fact that you have to have once loved someone to even begin to be truly capable of hating them. People often say that they hate certain comedians but they don't really – they just don't like their jokes or else are jealous of their success. I don't mind someone saying they hate me when I know they don't know who I am, but I can't bear someone who once loved me pretending that they don't hate me when I know they do.

But … did you lock the door?

Why does this always have to happen? It isn't just when I drive – I can be on foot or even with other people. One of my lowest points was asking a taxi driver to return to my house halfway along our journey to the train station so that I could be sure I had locked the door. I can still hear the surprise in his voice now: *'Go back, mate? Really?'* I told him I had forgotten my passport so that he wouldn't think I was weird, but I felt bad anyway. Having to invent a fictional short-haul trip to France to cover the fact I had so little luggage with me was no mean feat either. Step forward the fictitious 'sick relative', no more questions asked. Besides, he was glad of the extra fare, I am sure.

My fear comes from years of living alone, with no one but me to take responsibility for my mistakes. If I don't do

something, it doesn't get done – it is as simple as that. I absolutely refuse to go back this time though, no way. Things have changed. Each day I retrace my steps a number times, to check whether or not doors and windows have been locked, fridges closed, lights turned off, and each time I do so I find that I've always done what I thought I hadn't. I have to accept that I am a worrier and I do not forget to do things like locking the door – that is what other people do, people who aren't trying as hard as I am. But then again perhaps I have lulled myself into a false sense of security this time. Perhaps this time the door really is unlocked and I will be making a mistake if I don't go back. It would be worse to have stopped and decided to carry on than not to have considered the possibility at all. Once my neighbour knocked on my door to tell me that I had left my car window down, so I *am* unreliable. Admittedly it was years ago now and nothing bad happened as a result, but still it sows seeds of doubt in my mind – you only have to fail once to be a failure. If I wait here any longer I will have wasted as much time as I would have by going back to check whether the door was locked after all. I have to make a decision.

I think you left it open, because you rushed down the driveway to put the bin bag in the wheelie bin and forgot to go back and lock the door.

Now, that seems plausible; I absolutely could have done that. A few net curtains twitch around me to

43

remind me that I am disturbing the order of things, as if the houses themselves are winking at me in sly warning, like a Cockney down a dark alley, though in truth it is simply the inquisitiveness of the people behind who have nothing better to worry about than whether a stranger is in their midst.

I have lived in Swindon for five years now, and to me it is something of a Goldilocks town, in that it is just the right size for what I need. If it were any bigger, decision-making would be rendered utterly impossible by having too many options for which shop/restaurant/post office to use. Equally, any smaller and it would make impossible the chances of disappearing into a shapeless crowd when out and about.

This is a town where you might recognise faces but never need to know names. The kind of place where you can be 'the guy who is always in the chip shop at the same time as me on a Friday' but need never become 'Alan, who is married to Sarah, who used to work at the Cash and Carry but lost his job because he was caught sniffing women's shoes in the changing rooms so now works from home but really is supported by Sarah because he's too embarrassed to leave the house because he knows we spend most of our time talking about him and will do until something happens to someone else whose life need not affect us save for the fact we have so little else to talk about.'

44

People who have lived here all their lives will tell you that the traffic is bad or that crime is worse than it used to be, but those of us who have had experience of living in bigger cities will tell you that the traffic is rarely beyond manageable and, if you didn't scour the local newspaper on a daily basis, you would barely notice the petty crime that goes on. I lived in Bristol long enough to see that Swindon is actually a fairly quiet place. I left five years ago because the people I was living with had seen too much of my weakness for them to have the respect for me I wish for. The city echoed with mistakes I had made and everywhere the memories of failures I made earlier made it difficult for anything to seem perfect ever again. I wonder if there will ever be a place I can foresee spending the rest of my life in. More likely it is me who will change; one day I will stop caring about the mistakes of the past. Hopefully.

Swindon is, I'll grant you, an odd place to decide to build your utopia, but it seemed right at the time. House prices are as low as anywhere in the region, transport links make it an easy place to get out of and, most importantly of all, I don't know anyone here. The door need never knock unexpectedly on a quiet Sunday and force me into a state of begrudging hospitality. I have a home phone, but no one but me knows the number. You might think this pointless, but I adore it. It makes the phone a talisman of my self-imposed isolation – I

am like Willy Wonka, but I make no sweets and the closest I get to an army of Oompa Loompas is the occasional spider infestation. *Oompa Loompa doopedy doo, I've got a Dyson hoover for you!*

Most of the time I adore this solitude though I must confess that illness brings home with shocking clarity how, despite living in a large town and having neighbours on either side of me, it is possible to feel tremendously isolated by my choices. Recently a bad meat and potato pie sent me into feverish convulsions, my body going into full evacuation mode to rid itself of the pollutants inside. It was then that I became aware that there was nobody close enough to me to bring round warm soups, to mop my brow, or (in the worst-case scenario) discover my shrivelled up corpse on the bathroom floor. Twenty-eight is too young to be one of those people whose bodies lie undetected for weeks before questions are raised. 'Here lies Jon Richardson. He died of a pie. Ashes to ashes, crust to crust. RIP.'

When I left my last home in Bristol, I thought for a long time about moving to the seaside, but I am not yet old enough to spoil that surprise. Like hearing Christmas adverts in October, nobody should live by the sea until they are old enough to appreciate it – its smells and its sounds. The sea is there to remind us what insignificant pieces of shit we all are. When you start to worry about death and how the world will cope without you, the sea roars its laughter down on the sands of your concern and tells you that it will be around long after you and was here long before you. You have to be old enough to appreciate this, having acquired the intelligence and perspective not to misinterpret this as a threat, rather than the arm across the shoulder it really is. 'Don't worry old friend. The sands over which you walk are made up of the very bones of things that once, like you, worried about what would become of them. Now you carry them away with you in your shoes and they find their way into the corners of your kitchen and bury themselves deep into your living room carpet. They have no more to worry about, but I am here still.'

I have always felt like the larger coastal towns had a latent aggression about them, almost as if the inhabitants were still worried about invasion by sea so walked around with broken bottle tops and concealed knives just in case. Because of the prevalence of old people seeking to die with sand in their socks, the young, for fear of being typecast as living in a glorified nursing home, start drinking blue drinks as soon as they finish work and take drugs as if to prove to 'them London fuckers' that they know how to have a good time, too.

The sea, however, doesn't care. No matter what they do to try and impress it or repel its advances, it lurches forward and eases back with comic consistency, as if it

is playing a game of chicken with those who live inland; a show of power that one day, if they look like they have forgotten to flinch, it might not retreat as soon as it should.

Of course not all elderly people retreat to the sea in their final years. There is an elderly couple who live on my boring little street in Swindon and that makes me feel sorry for them. It isn't that we live in a particularly bad area, but just that it isn't particularly nice either. It was built for people like me who could just about live anywhere, so long as it has four walls to put a bed and a toilet in. If Travelodge made towns, they would make Swindon. It does the job quite happily, thank you. *Quite* happily. Our local pub is a perfect example of this desire not to exceed sufficiency. It serves beer and has been built with aged beams to belie its newness, but it has none of the soul of a good pub. The ceiling would once have been white but has clearly not been repainted since the smoking ban came into place, and as such carries the trademark yellowy-orange patchiness. Perhaps I am wrong and the patchiness exists because the pub ends each night with a lock-in for selected clientele who sit around drinking ale and laughing heartily whilst smoking cigars, but I doubt it. People go there to do what they need to do, to drown what needs to be drowned and go home. Above the bar are a number of brass plaques engraved with playful re-imaginings of well-known phrases and proverbs.

'A friend in need is a bloody nuisance'

'Where there's a will, there's a dead relative'

And my particular favourite: *'If arseholes could fly, this would be an airport'*

Then, in the middle of the bar, right above the new and ostentatious pump for a well-known lager, which rises up like a serpent from the bar and seems to point upwards at the laminated piece of card, crudely printed from a computer in a number of different colours now faded with time:

The Customer is always Right. A Right pain in the Arse.

This last one doesn't even really work – it is simply rude, another way of telling anyone on the wrong side of the bar that they are not welcome here. I don't know why they don't just go the whole hog and write 'FUCK OFF' in huge letters above the front door. Of course they are jokes, we can enjoy these signs because we are safe in the knowledge that we are polite and generous customers, and it is understood that the staff will be happy to attend to our every whim with a smile. Except that they aren't, and we aren't. The customers here are tired and rude, the staff not much better. It takes the gloss off the wit and all that is left is a sense of begrudging service.

Drink here if you must, but know this ... I absolutely hate your guts. If you die on the property I will call for medical assistance, as is my duty, but should you fall even one pace outside my front door, I will simply laugh and be glad that you won't be returning any time soon.

My street has no more character, with nothing to mark it out from any of the others around except for the words written on the signpost at the top of the road. All the streets round here are named after famous wartime actors. Classy. The houses are all identical and this ensures that the happiness of the occupants is entirely down to them. British people talk a lot about 'keeping up with the Joneses', trying to match your neighbours' possessions: cars, hanging baskets, new windows. When the new-build houses are all identical it shaves off another layer of your potential individuality, which is absolutely fine by me.

There are clues as to who lurks behind the walls of the individual houses, if you care to look for them, such as the ostentatious pebbledashing of the retired couple down the road, keen to show that their wealth has not been hit by recent economic troubles. I have no problem with pebbledashing in the right place, but I'm afraid here it simply looks as though a drunk snowman has been sick all over their home whilst staggering back from the pub. Twice a year, at Halloween and

Christmas, houses containing young children are made obvious by the volumes of cheap plastic paraphernalia that adorn the walls and front garden. From inflatable waving Santas to witches on broomsticks hanging from the guttering, the cartoon exteriors belie the misery and squabbling going on behind them. The children always look bruised from the inside out and the parents exhausted by what they are sure was once love.

And then there is my house. Plain and grey, there are no plants on the tarmacked driveway since I am never at home long enough to look after them. I have a wheelie bin, thank the council, and a little porch light whose bulb has never worked as long as I have lived there. I don't get many visitors anyway, so it is of no use really. The point of moving to Swindon was to encourage me to make more of an effort to travel to see my friends and family who are spread out across the country, which I do my best to do, although it seems harder year on year to find time when days off coincide.

Swindon is a place in which I can exist in the meantime, drinking and sleeping. It's not that I am unhappy here, just that happiness simply isn't a factor. In the same way that you need the pang of hunger to appreciate full satiety, you need happy days in the park to appreciate the blues. There is nothing like that here, just people getting on with what they need to do and trying not to think about it too much. I don't mean to

make this sound depressing, because it isn't really – it's just the way it is. Cavemen didn't waste their time thinking about whether or not they were happy or whether their lives had meaning; they were out hunting and trying to stay alive. We're the same creatures – nothing has changed that much. We invented happiness when finding food became too easy and survival became the norm.

Once we could all get through the days without trying, we had to find some other reason to wake up each morning; we had to adopt a scoring system to see who was winning at being alive – happiness! Now we think about it all the time, we talk about it with our partners and we travel the world in search of it. I am playing a much longer game; like good comedy I believe the secret to be about timing. If I am too happy in my youth, then my senior years will surely see me unhappily lamenting the passing of the life I once had. If, however, I maintain a level of enforced melancholy for as long as possible, then I can escape into retirement rather than be forced into it. If the last day of my life is the happiest, that will suit me just fine.

As I ponder this point, a miserable-looking old woman walks by my car with bags full of shopping and stares at me as she passes, distrustful of why I am parked on her street and completely unaware that I live just around the corner. Her latent hatred of me

is typical of almost everyone I encounter here. My neighbours, I am quite sure, suspect that I am a serial killer, a view I am quite happy to promote whenever I get the chance if it keeps them from talking to me, be it with a well-timed sinister chuckle to myself, or by making sure that they see how meticulously I clean the interior carpets of my car.

I must point out at this juncture that I am not a killer, though I have often thought about it when in crowded cinema screenings or on public transport – but who amongst us can honestly say that they haven't? There is no reason for them to think this of me, save for the fact that if you asked them to describe my character they would most likely tell you any combination of the following:

1. I am polite
2. I am hard working
3. I am always well presented and meticulous
4. I keep myself to myself
5. I wouldn't say boo to a goose

As any viewer of late-night crime documentaries will be able to testify, this is a classic serial-killer profile. It only takes a few bad pennies to ruin things for everyone and it's thanks to the likes of Jeffrey Dharmer that men like myself are eyed with suspicion wherever we

go. I am no saint, of course, and willingly confess that while I may not have said boo to a goose, I did tell a swan to 'fuck off' during a walk in the Lake District a couple of years back.

The car's fan kicks in as the engine has been idling for too long now and my mind is turned back to the issue in hand. The problem, you see, is that taking the rubbish out is a rare event since I spend so little time at home, and so I am apt to remember doing it. Locking doors, however, is something I do all the time, so each individual occurrence blurs into an obscurity of infinite replicas. Perhaps if I mark out each time as unique by saying something memorable as I do it, it might stick better in my memory:

'Jon Richardson is locking his front door in the rain and he had Shreddies for breakfast. Boobs.'

That kind of thing would be memorable. This is what I will do from now on, but this time I am just going to drive and when I get back tomorrow and find that the door was locked the whole time, I will treat myself to a smug, self-satisfied smile and know that I am getting better at life. In weeks and years gone by I would have gone back to check, but that was when I didn't have Gemma to think about.

Gemma is the reason I am trying to be more normal, because I imagine that's what she wants me to be. The best dating advice I can give you is that women like

54

men who aren't weird – and, I suppose, vice versa – and that's probably where I have been going wrong for the last eight years. I am not a particularly attractive man, shorter than I would like and with too round a head to feel entirely comfortable when walking past a tennis court, but nor am I ugly enough to warrant the eight-year suspension from the opposite sex that I have been serving. My voice is rather too shrill and I tend to moan too much, but I suspect the main problem has been things like checking doors and getting uncomfortable because I feel that I have stepped on more cracks in the pavement with my left foot than my right – that's what has marked me out for singledom. No one wants to walk the streets arm in arm with a man who occasion-ally breaks free to cross the road and step on a grid to 'even things out'.

Having someone else to think about once more holds a light up to some of my more eccentric behaviours and I can see that parking by the roadside, yards from your house, and sitting in a catatonic state is not right. Life is about simply playing the odds and I have to concen-trate on making myself a reliable target for love. Gemma and I are normal people and we go about our business normally, thinking about one another all the while. Besides, who would call at my house even if the door were unlocked? Swindon and its total isolation wins again!

Mirror, signal, manoeuvre. As I finally set off to my gig, I sing a song of victory to myself, a victory over the old me.

Hit the road, Jon, and don't you go check that door.

13.02

THE MIGHWAY CODE

Approaching Birmingham I am finally starting to calm down and truly forget about things back in Swindon. For the first half an hour I realised that I had been kidding myself if I thought I could just drive away and not suffer any repercussions. The hardest moment came when I stopped for petrol, by which time I had not only become convinced that I left the door unlocked, but also wide open. I pictured vividly a burglar very casually walking up my stairs and taking my big TV from the living room, the closest thing I have to a friend in Swindon, before sauntering back out again and smiling at my next-door neighbour as he loaded it into the back of his van with all his other, much more hard-fought booty. The neighbours would, of course, do nothing.

Well, he can't be a thief because he is so brazen and the door isn't forced. Jon must be moving away to another town … Good! Stinking murdering paedo with his closed curtains and clean car.

My paranoia is simply because my SkyPlus recording system means that my television is now more reliable than any girlfriend I have ever had. In the days
when you had to ask a partner to record *Match of the
Day* for you, a really good one might remember nine
times out of ten, but there would always be a time when
they forgot, or couldn't find a tape, or the time it had
come on ten minutes earlier because there was no
lottery so they missed the first match (the best match)
because they were still watching *Four Weddings and a
Funeral* on the other side. But with modern technology,
one press of a button ensures that whatever the day,
whatever the time, your favourite shows are always
waiting for you and nothing is ever expected of you in
return. If my television could make me a cup of tea in
the morning and put it by my bed, and could drive me
home from the pub when I am drunk, I would marry it
instantly – though I might need to get a coaxial attachment for my penis. The TV really is enormous; stupidly
large, given the size of my living room. I can never
quite get far back enough to see what's on all of it, but
it's good for watching football on. You can see why I
would become so afraid of the thought of losing it all
through sheer carelessness. Those feelings have now
subsided.

Aside from having to concentrate on not having an
accident caused by the lunacy of some drivers, I find

driving to be an incredibly relaxing experience. I never feel more free than when behind the wheel of my car. It is only our autopilot that makes us turn left where we are supposed to and take the correct exit at a roundabout. The truth is that every time you get into your car there are an almost infinite number of possibilities open to you, and it is now possible to drive from the northernmost tip of Scotland to China and therefore anywhere in between! When you realise that this is possible, you cannot help but ask how many decisions you actually make in your life. By a decision made, I mean a conscious effort to take control of a situation rather than simply allowing yourself to respond in what you think is the correct way, given your track record and how you are perceived by the people around you.

Compared with this number, then ask yourself how many things just seem to happen? How many times have you got to work and been unable to remember quite how you got there, or gone through an entire week of your brief life without feeling as though you have done anything significant? In order to be absolutely sure that where you are going is the right choice you first have to consider and discount every other option available to you at that point. Would going to Tuscany make you happier than going to Asda? Would it make you happier in the short term but create

problems in the long term, or is it a viable option for a permanent relocation? What about Munich? Of course you don't do this; no one can live their life according to this set of guidelines or none of us would get anything done for spending our time thinking about the alternatives, but isn't the very fact that there are that many alternatives in itself a wonderfully refreshing thought? Sometimes it can seem as if there are none, when in fact nothing could be further from the truth. You just have to wake yourself up to noticing them, but most of us don't.

I know that while I am almost certain to end up at my gig in Yorkshire, if I were to just keep on *not* taking the correct turn then I would be bound to end up somewhere unexpected. From the age of ten I remember being driven to school by my mum and feeling a nervous cramping in my stomach, a pressure that existed precisely because I had always been academically very successful up until that point. I had always done well in tests and exams, behaved well and done all my homework but even then to me that just meant that the one day it all collapsed around me everybody would laugh at me all the more. Teachers would be more disappointed in me than anyone else.

We thought you were one of the good ones, but you aren't. You've let us all down by forgetting that calculator. What a pity.

There were brief moments of escapism from that tension inside me every few hundred yards though, brought on by the thought that one day my mum would look at me and my sister and say: 'Look, I don't want to go to work, you don't want to go to school, so shall we just head off? I'm going to keep on going straight ahead and if you feel like we should take a turn, tell me and we will. We'll just stop when we get hungry and nobody will ever be able to find us again.'

I think I could see that urge too, in her eyes, but whatever pressures were on me, a ten-year-old boy, to do what was expected of me, they must have been on her, a college head of department with two children, a hundred times over. How do we build these lives for ourselves? It was right to stay; that's what people do – they don't just run away as appealing as it may seem for a brief moment.

To this day, in the back of my car I keep a sleeping bag beside a shoebox containing a box of cereal bars, a bottle of red wine (with a screw top – you only make that mistake once) and a pot noodle – my own emergency kit should I one day have the courage to drive myself somewhere new, where nobody knows where I am, and start hiding from the world. This is hardly the same as burning all my savings and hitchhiking my way into the Canadian wilderness, but I like to think of myself in some small way as a part of what I call the

Boot Generation. All we need is the air in our lungs, the wind in our hair, and the dried noodle snack we can have when we eventually find a kettle and a plug socket. The man can't keep us down!

I glance down at the dashboard to check whether I have enough petrol to get me where I need to go, as I do roughly every five minutes or so, but I still have over two-thirds of a tank. I have seen so many films in which drivers glance down and see the needle edging into the red that I live in constant fear of that moment, because as we all know, that is when the murderer appears behind you.

I remind myself that I am not a Hollywood film star, nor am I a dippy student, driving across the Australian outback in a beaten up old car I bought from a gap-toothed simpleton having completed my final exams. I am driving a silver Ford Fiesta across England and I filled my car up at a local supermarket, gaining reward points in the process. I think this might make the world's dullest Hollywood movie, but that's fine with me. At this thought, a car whose driver wants to exit at the upcoming junction, but not enough to pay attention to how close it is, meanders across the motorway without indicating and pulls into the space I had left in front of me. Other people brake and swerve to avoid him but go no further, but I waste no time in slamming on my horn and when I can see his eyes meet mine in his

rear-view mirror I proudly extend my middle finger towards him. Only once this has been done do I stop to think about how big he might be, or how many other people might be with him. A mist descends when I am in my car, something to do with being encased in metal I suspect, which makes me feel less like a small, scrawny man and more like Robocop. I doubt Robocop would have had the commercial success he did had his voice been as camp as my car horn, but it is the only gesture I have to make.

There has been a slow and steady shift away from the traditional Highway Code over recent years, so gradual that most people haven't even realised it has happened. While the key points remain the same in that we drive on the left and go clockwise around roundabouts, most of the smaller 'rules' as they were known back then have changed and been replaced by guidelines. For the uninitiated, here are a few of the main alterations to the things you may have been taught when learning to drive which make up the brand new Mighway Code:

1. *Roundabouts:* When approaching a roundabout, be advised that whichever direction you intend to travel in, the correct lane is always the one in which there are the fewest other cars. Once at the front of the queue, note that if you wait every

time you see a car coming, you will never get anywhere. The thirty-second rule states that if you have been waiting for thirty seconds or more, you must move out immediately and other road users are legally obliged to make space for you. If, through no fault of your own, you miss your turning on a roundabout, be aware that simply going round once more, though it may only take a few seconds, will pump unwanted noxious gasses into an already suffocated atmosphere. You must do whatever you can to get across the traffic as soon as possible and back on course, reversing if needed.

2. *Signalling:* Indicating is a dangerous procedure since it involves removing your hands from the wheel and draws your attention away from driving safely. It should be avoided at all times (for exceptions see rule 3) as not only does it reduce the control that you have over your own car, there may be epileptics in front of or behind you who might be triggered into having a seizure by a sudden burst of flashing orange lights. As we know that speed is a killer, and light travels faster than sound, it is therefore advisable to use your horn instead of your indicators to alert other drivers to your presence.

3. *Parking:* Using what used to be known as 'hazard lights' makes it legal to park anywhere. Double yellow lines do not apply to anyone whose operation can be preceded by the word 'just'. For example, it is illegal to stop on double yellow lines to go to the bank, but it is not illegal to '*just* pop into the bank'. Double yellow lines also do not apply to big men with shaved heads driving transit vans. The 'I-know-you-are-you-said-you-are-but-what-am-I' rule states that calling a traffic warden a 'fucking parasite' renders his ticket useless with no comebacks times infinity. Traffic wardens are absolutely NOT trying to make it easier to park legally by deterring people from parking illegally; they are generating millions of pounds a second which is used to buy weapons for Middle Eastern despots. Fact.

4. *Motorway driving:* The only reason that driving into the back of someone causes damage is because of the gap between the cars which allowed sufficient speed to be built up – ergo gaps cause crashes. The safest thing to do on the motorway is to drive with your front bumper touching the rear bumper of the car in front, so that when they brake, your car will respond

instantly. The middle lane of the motorway is known as 'the driving lane' and all cars should gravitate towards this lane. The inside lane is a spare hard shoulder, for use by truck drivers and pussies. The outside lane or 'stud lane' is for businessmen who have important meetings to go to, or back home from. If you see any car other than an Audi, BMW or Mercedes in the stud lane then you must pull over and use the emergency phone to contact the emergency services.

5. *The speed limit:* It is a common misconception that the number shown in circular signs with a red border is the speed limit. The real speed limit is whatever is in the red circle plus ten per cent, plus five mph, plus your age. Anyone driving below that should be encroached and, if necessary, pushed along at the appropriate speed. The slower you drive, the longer you will be on the road and the more likely it is that you might have an accident or 'be accidented on' by someone else. Cut your journey times – put your foot down.

6. *The most important rule of the Mighway Code is this:* Accidents only ever happen to, or because of, other people. You are a great driver; it's all

these other pricks that ruin things for everyone else. That Jeremy Clarkson drives fast and he's still cool, right? Damn right. *Vroom vrooms. Neeeeooowwwm.* Maybe I could get a turret fitted to the front of my car then I could shoot baddies? (Make gun noise for an hour.)

Calming myself down and enjoying the sense of relief as the car in front veers off the motorway and onto the slip road without further incident or retaliation, I glance in my rear-view mirror, just to double-check that there isn't an ominous looking figure in a jet-black HGV 'riding my tail'.

But it's not a jet-black HGV. It's a pinkish-red car – maybe a Renault Clio. My brain once more decides to rush off into fantasy, rather than confront the tedious reality. Could it be Gemma at the wheel of the car behind, or perhaps the one behind that, trying to catch up with me before she and Papa discover that both of them are on illicit dates, he with his mistress, and Gemma with me, her mystery man? We are in Paris, city of lovers, and tonight we will be strolling along the Left Bank in the moonlight. In spite of all my previous fears and misgivings I now know that we are destined to be together. I am her nemesis and she is mine.

My heart misses a beat.

Maybe Gemma *is* my nemesis. How does she know where I am heading and when I left? She could be stalking me. Perhaps she even knows where I live. They say that in cities you're never more than a few feet away from a rat. Maybe Gemma is *my* rat, lurking and skulking in holes and corridors and behind doorways while I have been blithely ignorant of her presence? Perhaps even our meeting was not the chance encounter it seemed, but more chess play on her part.

How long has this been going on? It could be months! She probably has a secret cellar wallpapered with my photos and press cuttings and stained with my blood or even sperm that she stole from my GP when I last went for a medical. Of course she keeps a diary and logs my movements from hour to hour. She will no doubt think she knows me better than I do, and she's probably right.

Is she going to kill me? If she can't be with me, surely she will make sure nobody else will either. She may even be planning to *eat* me.

I cast another nervous glance into my rear-view mirror and let out a laugh as I see the face staring back at me. The woman behind is in fact a tiny, Sue Pollard-like woman with short brown hair and an overbite, fighting to control a red Nissan Micra. Her eyes are squinting through her huge glasses and she is hunched forward, holding on so tightly to the steering wheel that

it looks as though she expects it will fly off out of the window if she loosens her grip for even a split second.

I laugh because despite all the tension in her eyes and shoulders, she is mouthing the words to whatever song is playing on her stereo, her head moving sharply and with no rhythm whatsoever from side to side. It looks to me more like she is whispering some incantation to her spirit guide, or perhaps giving herself a stern talking to. Perhaps she is running out of petrol and the murderer is gaining on her ...

There is a different feeling about this drive, about why I am checking the distance between myself and Sue Pollard, and why I thought it might be Gemma, and why I got angry at the man who cut me up; a better feeling than usual. I am no longer simply getting angry for the sake of it, hating other people for making mistakes – I am trying to protect myself because *I am actually looking forward to the future.*

This might seem a perfectly normal emotion, but it isn't for me, or at least it hasn't been for the last few years. I am no longer just trying to avoid having an accident because of the inconvenience it might cause in terms of delayed journey time and forms to fill in, or my fear of pain, I am trying to stay alive for living's sake! I smile at the thought and feel my shoulders loosen and drop by at least an inch.

When I arrive I will check into my accommodation and text Gemma. Definitely.

And then another thought strikes me: I'd better text my agent as well about our meeting on Monday at the same time – just to make sure nothing goes wrong. He says big things are about to happen for me.

17.11

BE AND BE JUDGED

'I have a room booked in the name of Richardson.' I confirm to the well-presented, heavily perfumed landlady stood in the doorway in front of me. I saw her watching me park in her driveway through her living-room window, but she still made me ring the bell before she would come to the door. A pointless piece of posturing on her part which she feels puts her in charge, I suppose.

'Oh ... Right,' she almost questions, looking down at me in the way a nightclub bouncer might look down on a pleading sixteen-year-old boy who has drawn a biro-beard on his chin and worn his dad's best shirt, not noticing how poorly it hangs from his much smaller adolescent frame.

Against her will, she seems to concede that there is indeed a reservation made in this name, but there is something else in her eyes, or rather in her now furrowed brow ... a problem lurking underneath the surface. Back on my office desk, four and a quarter hours of motorway driving away, a tea-stained mug that I had forgotten about until Nottingham sits defiantly on an otherwise clean and uncluttered surface. I am not in the mood for any complications. An awkward few seconds pass.

Such is the glamour of life as a middle-of-the-range touring stand-up comedian in the current era, I find myself checking into a homely but very average B&B somewhere in Yorkshire, a place chosen by my agent. I have to confess I don't know exactly where I am, since my satnav directed me here, which I suppose all contributes to the feeling I have of somehow being here against my will.

Where possible I stay in large, faceless chain hotels where all the rooms look the same and I could describe in clear detail the layout and furnishings of the room before I even step inside. In places like these no one will notice if I don't turn up for breakfast or if I use more toilet roll than an average guest. For my part I don't care if there aren't any paintings of dogs in my room or doilies on the coffee table. I don't even care if the receptionist doesn't wish me 'a pleasant stay'; I just want to get upstairs and lock the door behind me (placing the 'Do Not Disturb' sign on the outside first) and hide from the world until I need to go out for my gig. Small, rural villages however tend not to house large hotels and so I am forced to stay in a B&B and have

tortured conversations with someone who I am paying money to in return for a service, but seems to want to assume the role of surrogate auntie and tell me all the things I can't do while I'm under her roof without apologising for any inconvenience or lack of tolerance.

'Richardson, yes. Is it just you?'

'Yes. That's right.'

'You've booked a double?'

'Yes.'

Another few seconds pass in silence and then her eyebrows are raised up an inch, taking the corners of her mouth up with them as hostages, forming a crude half-smile. 'Ah! I understand. Is someone meeting you later?'

By this she means to ascertain whether I am here as part of some sex cult or else a lonely businessman awaiting a visit from some sort of call girl. The tone has a kind of accusatory 'I've seen your sort before' ring to it and I am certain that this woman is, as we speak, incorrectly piecing together my entire life back story. Married too young when my girlfriend got pregnant due to my carelessness and sense of invulnerability, now she is at home looking after our child and crying silently into her breast pump while I travel the country with my job, bedding budget prostitutes in good, clean, family-run guest houses for kicks. People who live in small, prim villages such as this should not

be allowed to watch crime dramas set in East London unless they have passed an intelligence exam which proves that they will not assume that everyone who travels alone and comes from the south is a dangerous scumbag.

On more vulnerable days I have been known to invent a story at this stage to avoid suspicion – a wife who is unable to travel with me due to illness or because she is attending the local church service where she sings at the end and hands around a saucer. One day this bluff will be called by someone asking to see a photo or ask for a contact number for her in case of emergency, and I will get myself into serious trouble, the likes of which are only ever seen in poorly scripted sitcoms. On this occasion I am not in the mood to be judged, however, and am angry at her insinuation, so I play it out straight-faced.

'No,' I say curtly, 'it's just going to be me. On my own.'

'Oh. Why did you book a double then? Why didn't you book a single?'

In my mind she goes on … *What on earth do you need two sides of the bed for? To masturbate in one half and cry yourself to sleep in the other? Why don't you just leave people like me alone to get on with our lives instead of flaunting your immorality all over my clean, white sheets?*

74

I don't show any anger, because the bed and break-fast set-up is one that gives all the power to her. My status is no higher than that of visiting cousin, a pest but one that she is obliged to tolerate. 'I don't know,' I say. 'Call it a moment of reckless extravagance if you like.'

And then she laughs, almost. Though in truth it is more of a light-hearted exhalation than a genuine chuckle. 'Fair enough.' And with that she begrudgingly checks me in, tells me that breakfast will be served between 4.00 and 4.30 a.m. sharp, gives me a key for my room and one for the front door and asks me not to eat takeaway food within four hundred yards of the premises. She stops just short of telling me that Jesus is watching me and will punish me if I touch my nether regions in her en-suite shower room, but I know she is tempted. Trudging my suitcase up the stairs I reflect on how my life is littered with these kinds of conversations.

'Table for one is it, sir? Would you like this shitty one over in the corner by the toilets so everyone can stare at you at least once while you pretend to read your book for something to do other than confront your failure to find a mate?'

'Just one ticket for the show? Really? Shall I book you one at the back so you can sneak in quietly at the end and not feel embarrassed by yourself?'

Or the worst of all, 'No, I don't need the two-for-one offer thanks, I couldn't possibly manage two pizzas and would just end up throwing the other one away … No I don't have anyone to give the other one to, I don't know anyone in this area. No, no one.' These are the times when it feels that everyone in the world is in a relationship but me, and that is why my text to Gemma is of such paramount importance.

She is the trail of breadcrumbs leading me away from the witch's house; she is the future spent picnicking in our garden rather than eating off my lap in the back of my car. Right now she is the only positive train of thought in my mind and perhaps the pressure of not wanting to lose such a precious commodity is the reason I haven't yet texted her since she first gave me her number almost a week ago.

Sitting now on the end of my bed looking down at the eleven digits she scribbled on the top of my bill, I feel the same distress and trepidation that a mother looking down at the eleven digits on her newborn baby must feel. She works at a local carvery and we have been flirting quite successfully for a number of months now, a position in which I am entirely comfortable to stay. Most Sundays I go there for my dinner and our conversation flows easily in allotted ninety-second portions

between courses and we both laugh a great deal. Following an early and amusing misunderstanding in which she mistook tomato-sauce stains for blood, I have been maintaining the pretence that I am a travelling hitman and she has continued to giggle as if this is the funniest thing she could ever imagine.

When she laughs, all the cynicism I maintain in my professional life disappears and for that brief second it seems inconceivable that we could live any way but happily ever after. Her smile is truly wonderful and I am starting to think (in fact I am certain) that seeing her smile is the real reason I go to eat there once a week, and not for the chewy, grey meat and brutally overcooked broccoli whose florets could be rung out like a wet sponge.

Last Sunday was no exception and I ate an early lunch before driving to that night's show on the south coast, but what changed from our normal routine was that, after I paid, she brought back my change and receipt, upon which was written the words:

Next time you're in the area for 'business' why don't we both eat some food somewhere, rather than me just watching and bringing drinks? x

77

Business is what I call my killings, so that is a funny joke on her part and she has successfully avoided falling into the trap of using 'your' instead of 'you're', which is, if not an immediate red-card offence, certainly a yellow with a strong talking-to. I am in no doubt that if you use the term 'luv' in a letter or text message then you are incapable of truly understanding the emotion. Artists have not pored over heartache and unrequited sentimentality for years so that our generation could decide that four letters is simply one too many to express how we feel.

I have always thought that 'unrequited' is such a clinical and ugly word. Portraying none of its ability to devastate and define a person's life, it sounds rather more like the sort of word that should only ever be used by accountants and financiers. *'Looking over your figures from the fiscal year 2009 to 2010 I note that there was an unaccounted-for fluctuation in your unrequited assets. Could you tell me why this was?'*

Getting the number and watching her blush as she gave it to me stirred up emotions I have successfully repressed for the last eight years: a flushed face, electric nervous excitement, a slight need for a wee and everything else. This should all have been a good thing, I know, and would be considered to be nothing less by most sane people. A girl I like has shown that she likes me back – *bingo*. To me, however, it potentially

represents the end of the only perfect stage of our relationship. No longer can we just go on flirting and both imagining the other to be all that is missing from our lives; now my hand has been forced, the beehive has been punched square in the face and things are going to change, most likely for the worse. The more time she spends with me, the more she will come to realise that I am actually quite a tedious man, difficult to spend time with, and eventually I will lose the one thing I look forward to each week – our Sunday flirtation.

The sad fact is that I will lose that privilege whether I choose to meet up with her or not, as the other option is to not phone her, never go back to the restaurant and eventually move away to avoid an embarrassing encounter with her and a new boyfriend in the street. But I'm not going to phone anyway, I am going to send a text. I am going to, because I really like her and I need to realise that this is a good thing. So I will text her. Soon.

I want it to be known that in no way am I maintaining any time between receiving her number and getting in contact because I think it will make me look cool; far from it – I would have called her from the car park of the restaurant if I thought I could have found the right words. Clearly it is probably a little late for a man who dines alone every Sunday in a crummy carvery to play the cool card, so the plucky loser card is the only one I

have left. All week I have been arguing with myself over what to say and have already deleted several drafts of the message that seemed either not funny enough, 'funny but trying too hard to be funny' or didn't successfully convey how keen I am on her. The first drafts went roughly like this:

> Hey Gemma. Hope the rest of your shift went quickly. I'd love to go for some food at some point. Do you have anywhere in particular in mind? J

By abbreviating my name from Jon to just 'J' I think I was hoping to add some informality to proceedings but then decided I was just being too vague and making myself sound like a member of a shit boy band. It also occurred to me that she could have given her number out several times this week, to a James, a Joe and a Jeremy as well as to me. Nothing would crush my early affections like a reply that read, 'Excuse me, but who is this?' Urgh. I shudder just to think of it. Referring to her job also seemed somehow disingenuous. I want her to know that I consider her to be more than a waitress to me. Deleted. The second batch of texts were as follows:

Hello! I'd love to take you for dinner at
some point, when is good for you? Jon
(P.S. Do you know what gets blood out
of cashmere?) x

The x always got deleted straight away – what was I
trying to pull off there? Next in line for the cull was the
exclamation mark at the beginning, which made it
seem as though I was shouting at the poor girl like a
lunatic through a bus window. The blooded cashmere
line was supposed to be a joke, but what if she didn't
get it? Well then, I suppose she isn't right for me if she
doesn't get my crappy jokes, since that is (unfortunately) a large part of who I am. 'Take you for dinner'
also seemed a bit domineering. Perhaps she likes to pay
half?

Finances aside, the fact that she initiated the whole
thing by giving me her number means I suppose that
she is taking me out for dinner, and I am just going
along with the whole thing. Why can't it just be the last
century in which we could have liked each other from
afar for a few years before an etiquette breakdown at a
dance involving incorrect consumption of a vol-au-
vent meant we could never be seen together again and
one of us died of something horrific a few years later?

Curiously this is always my ideal relationship
scenario – the fleeting, unfulfilled passion with none of

the reality of life, in which we may steal a few short moments of happiness in our achingly brief encounter. The reality of life is proving to be more and more over-rated to me and perhaps to others, too. This may explain why in most UK homes, living room seating points towards the plasma screen in the corner rather than the room's other occupants. Which reminds me – someone is stealing my TV. I definitely left the pissing door unlocked. I'll text her later.

19.54

FIESTA TIME

Saturday night, I feel the air is getting hot. Steam is fogging the windows and the air is damp and close and stings my nostrils. Unlike for Whigfield, it isn't the heat rising from writhing bodies in a dark and sexy club I can feel, but the steam from the tray of hot chips I am eating off the back of a road atlas settled on my chest in my battered old Ford Fiesta, secluded behind a wall in a car park at the back of a theatre in Bradford. Nobody can see me inelegantly stuffing my face, with my seat reclined so far back that my eyes are level with my steering wheel, but looking out I am able to spy on all the revellers staggering into town on their hunt for what used to be love but now is nothing more than a night of grotesque exchanging of bodily fluids designed to cushion the impact of a lonely trawl through from Monday to Friday.

In spite of the drizzle, people are heading out in their finest weekend livery, hair washed and nails clipped, with good intentions I am sure, but secretly knowing (but never admitting to themselves) that they will more than likely be going home with someone they don't really find attractive, whose breath is a little meatier than they would like and who they will probably never again speak to beyond tomorrow morning's awkward pillow banter. This is a world I have gladly left behind me. It isn't that my current lifestyle choice is perfect, by any means, but I never feel better about the decisions I have made than now, hiding in my car before going to do my gig, watching the animals escaped from the zoo.

My rudimentary understanding of the dating techniques of prehistoric man, though I freely admit they may be too heavily influenced by cartoonists, are that he would simply beat a woman over the head and drag her back to his cave when the mood took him. I can't see that all that much has changed. Here, at what for us is the end of our supposed evolution, we use alcohol to drug the senses instead of physical violence, but we still call it 'going clubbing'. Young girls stagger around in heels so impractical as to render them useless in terms of the basic function of a shoe, as gracelessly as baby seals on the Canadian Gulf. The 'music' from the club behind the theatre in which I am to perform is also a violent attack on the tranquillity I crave.

While I recognise that female company is nice, I refuse to believe that clubbing is how people are supposed to meet to establish relationships on a level

far beyond what we consider to be a norm in modern society. I think I would have been far better suited to living some time in the 1940s, just after the war perhaps. Spirits high, a statistical advantage for a man looking to find a woman and a healthy dose of stuffiness and formality to add to any social occasion.

Were Gemma and I to have met one another under such conditions as those before me now, and were we to get married and have children, how could I possibly explain this to our grandchildren when they ask how granny and granddad got together? Gathered round the hearth on a wet Sunday afternoon, the children's big round eyes staring up at me as I switch off the Grand Prix and begin my tale:

'Well, young Sally! Granny and I were out at a nightclub, absolutely *shitfaced* I hasten to add' [cheeky giggle and look at Gran who is playing her now antiquated Nintendo DS in the corner, knitting having become extinct long ago], when our two friends at the time starting copping off with one another.

'Well as you can imagine this put Granny and I in a quite sticky social situation – as we've barely said two words to one another – but this was the new millennium and we weren't going to let that bother us! So … we downed another bottle of Blue Generic Alcohol each and headed back to ours for some old-fashioned sexual intercourse. I was too drunk to use a condom

and she was too drunk to care and that's how your mummy was born!

'We've been together ever since, because financially it made more sense for us to get family benefits than for me to have to pay child benefit *and* work, and although really we resent each other terribly and spend most of our days fantasising about the lives we could have led apart, we're now terrified of the alternative and too afraid of dying alone to think about change. OK, love? Stop crying and climb into your purpose-built three-dimensional entertainment unit.'

Perhaps this is how all our grandparents got together, but when asked they simply concoct lies about barn dances and having to be home before eleven to avoid a good hiding in order to save face. I probably have to stop thinking about things in terms of how they will look years down the line, or at least I am frequently told that I have to, but that just feels like admitting defeat.

Gemma would certainly be somewhat intimidated if she knew that a man who hadn't so much as sent her a text message yet had already broken the hearts of her grandchildren. This is my instinctive reaction, to allow the fact that Gemma and I might not have the chance of being together for the rest of our lives to be an excuse not to act in the short term. If I think we are going to break up at some point then I don't want to even get together. If I told you before a game of football that you

would have the best game of your entire life, score the most amazing goal ever seen in amateur football, but in the 89th minute you would suffer a horrendous leg break that might end your football career altogether, would you still play? Of course not, so I'm right then. My fondness for her now is no guarantee of long-term survival. I told my last girlfriend I was in love with her, and I meant it too. I am not in love with her any more, so I have to conclude that my feelings were temporary and I am fickle. The only honest answer when someone asks you if you love them is 'at the moment, yes', but try saying that without getting a kick in the chaps.

It is the sheer number of bodies swarming outside the club that strikes me. In much the same way that being in traffic on a motorway reminds me of how many cars must be on all the roads of the world at that point, spewing their noxious gases skyward, looking at this nightclub queue outside a grotty venue in Bradford makes me doubt the likelihood of any of us finding 'the one' if they do exist. There are simply too many people in the way. How am I to believe Gemma is Miss Right when there are millions upon millions of possible Miss Wrongs to check first?

In the long ago past, there would have been a choice of only two mates in a village. If a member of the opposite sex was roughly your age and unwed, you two would be together, end of story. These days, with the

advent of internet dating, one could easily believe that 'the one' for you lives on a remote farm in Papua New Guinea. Good luck finding them! It is said that there is someone out there for each of us, and I would hope that anyone who has walked through a town centre on a Saturday night would agree with me that this is indeed a crying shame. Some people need to be told that they need to polish up their act before they can find an audience for it.

I am most jealous when I see people who have found a way of sharing an unadulterated happiness in circumstances I could not tolerate. Hideous drunkards, scoffing ambiguous meats from a polystyrene tray in grotty, wet town centres, hand in hand and exchanging passionate kisses every twenty yards, are experiencing a happiness beyond judgement or self-awareness that I will simply never know. My mind turns to one such couple, witnessed walking home along a quiet street in Brighton one night, and utterly unaware of my presence behind them. Both smelled equally as bad as each other, were equally drunk and so were equally enraptured by the other.

'When we get home … hic … burp …' began the gentleman to his beloved, stumbling in a different direction with each word – the words came one by one, not flowing like liquid but cascading out of his mouth like glasses sliding off a wonky table and smashing on

to the floor. 'When we get … home … I'm gonna put you on that kitchen floor … and sp*nk all over ya!'

As another small part of me died inside, she giggled erotically and turned away from her trough of recently grilled animal carcass with lashings of chilli sauce to kiss him in the facial region.

Perhaps that's what women like, I thought. *Perhaps I should be threatening to do that to someone. But in a food preparation area? Never.*

The memory is enough to put me off the thought of ever being romantically involved with anyone ever again. As a football fan I feel as though I bear a responsibility for the misdemeanours of the players who represent the sport I love. Equally, by continuing my search for the woman of my dreams, I endorse this kind of behaviour. Staying single is my way of rejecting the whole charade, of somehow elevating myself above sexual deviance, above deception and heartbreak.

Besides, a thought has begun to germinate in the back of my mind for which staying single is not just the sad condition of my existence but might conceivably be a positive bonus – no, more than that, the necessary requirement … you could almost say the unique selling point.

Maybe, just maybe, there's a book in all this.

Maybe I can persuade a publisher that the very real issues that beset my life, my unbearable, deplorable

perfectionism, my militantly negative tendencies, which are already an apparently endless source of the material that feeds my stand-up act, could also be harnessed into service in writing a book about the Unbearable Darkness Of My Being, the impossibility of my finding true love and the reason why I'm still irredeemably single.

The problem with that idea of course is Gemma. If by some miracle I were to start seeing her, form a relationship and make it work, I would be quite unable to stand by the authenticity of my 'single and impossible' status. If I were to fulfil my dreams of becoming a writer, specialising in the area in which I am uniquely qualified to write, I would have to forfeit any chance of happiness with Gemma.

Yet the only way I could test this contradiction would be by pursuing both goals. It is of course quite possible that I might not get either the girl or the book contract, but it is quite clear that if I were to find true love, or any kind of love, my credibility as someone for whom happiness with another is impossible would be blown and I'd have to pay back my advance, which by now in my mind I have already spent on buying myself a secret *pied à terre* hidden away somewhere in the Lake District where my legions of adoring fans and readers could not possibly find me.

This obviously needs a little more thinking about. I jot a few notes in my diary and think about mailing a proposal to my agent.

As I step out of the car to walk across to the theatre, I press the button on my key and the door locks pleasingly with a sound of sliding metal followed by a thud. I say aloud:

'Jon Richardson is locking his car to prevent the rutting beasts from breaking into his car and stealing his Pot Noodles.'

I turn away and notice a man parked alongside me, staring up in disbelief at the antics of the weirdo who commentates on his entire life as if it were a football match. I guess I won't be forgetting whether or not I have locked the door on this occasion.

SUNDAY

07.58

QUEASY LIKE A SUNDAY MORNING

Any second … now? No. I am a 'mourning person'. Not because anybody close to me has recently passed away, but because I use that term to describe my demeanour at daybreak and as a way of separating myself from what are known as 'morning people' – those high-functioning, grinning morons who skip out of their beds and pounce at the dawn as eagerly and as energetically as a young puppy greets a hanging shoelace.

My mornings are (with the exception of Christmas Day) dark and sombre affairs, spent grieving for the sleep of which I have been robbed; morning is when blades of daylight hack viciously at the dreams that have kept you company throughout the night. Avoiding breakfast in here is not an option; she will know I have come back and will use my indolence as further ammunition to hate me, but right now toast and coffee seems a pathetic defence against everything the world has in store. It doesn't help that I have a hangover.

It's the morning after to end all others: Sunday. Where yesterday I could sit in my car and feel superior to those single people driven to the streets to find love in alleyways and behind skips, this morning paints an altogether different view of what it is to be in a relationship. Sundays are for the happy few who believe themselves to have found that person; whether it turns out that they are right or wrong, this morning it is enough simply to believe. A bed and breakfast brings all the discomfort of waking up in someone else's house, but with none of the fond memories of conquest of the night before. All around the country I imagine couples who are now being woken up by energetic children keen to start the day. Some will spend all morning in bed listening to Radio 4 – the omnibus edition of *The Archers*, followed by *Desert Island Discs*. Others will be heading out to their favourite café to enjoy breakfast over a newspaper before a walk home through the park. This is an idealised version of what it is to wake up in a relationship, of course, but today I feel like chasing ideals and pitying myself – such is my own Sunday routine! All the sense of isolation of being stuck on a desert island but without the delusion that anyone cares enough to ask after me, let alone what records I would take along. Although this morning feels different for two very clear reasons: one of which is Gemma and the other is the noise from next door.

Any second … now? No.

I have been staring at the clock and trying to predict when the numbers will change for the last six minutes without success. The digital time display reads 07:58 but, I realise, with no curves. An 8 is supposed to be a round number, smooth and squidgy.

Two fat ladies. 88.

But somehow these ladies have been mutated into a form where their sides are now pressed flat and yet still I understand them to be women. My mind conjures an image of two enormous Beryl Cook-style women, dressed in blue polka-dot dresses, and stuck in individual phone boxes. The frame of the door forms the digital number eight in my mind and the flesh of the women is pressed hard up against the glass; there is no space to breathe inside and their faces are filled with alarm.

How can I never have called into question before the ability of seven small lines to express numbers like 0 and 8 accurately, and who was so arrogant as to have come up with the idea in the first place? Then I start to wonder how my mind can have wandered so far from anything important to this trivial nonsense, so early?

Across the room on the desk sits a neatly scribed 'To do' list for the day and item number one 'Wake up' is waiting to be ticked off with a big fat swipe of the marker pen. Of course I don't think waking up is

anything to be proud of – in fact it is the very least I expect from each day of my life, but I put it on the list simply so that before I am even out of bed I have achieved a goal and can bathe in the appropriate sense of self-satisfaction. The very opening of my eyes ceases to be a mere inevitability and becomes one less thing that has to be done before I can slip back into my cocoon at night. However, there is a slight risk that by marking getting up as an achievement I am somewhat tempting fate. It would be sad enough for a family member to come across my body in a state of eternal slumber without them then having to go to my desk and see that my death was not only a tragedy but also a failure to execute a seemingly simple task.

Tsk! He couldn't even manage to get up. Pretty pathetic really. And now I suppose Muggins here will have to plan his funeral on top of everything else I have to do!

In one minute the alarm clock over my right shoulder will burst into life, giving me a further one minute to adjust my thoughts before getting out of bed at exactly eight o'clock and heading downstairs for an awkward communal breakfast. Most people think that when they set their alarm for eight o'clock, they 'get up at eight', but you don't – you get up after eight; you get up late without even knowing it. If you do not begin the day right on schedule, how can you possibly hope to

cope adequately with the rest of it, playing catch up as you are?

This morning, as it happens, I do not need my premature alarm nor my one minute's grace as I have already been awake long enough to watch the last seven minutes slip by without incident. A couple of cars have passed by me on the street outside, their lights breaking through the gaps in the slats of the window blind and dragging a neat linear pattern across the wall from the far right-hand side of the room towards the left, fading almost completely by the time it reaches my face in the dead centre.

The reason I woke up, or rather was woken up, seven minutes early is the noise coming from the wall behind me. Whoever is sharing the room next door, they are already arguing, somewhere about four feet behind my head, their own miserable bed mirroring my own 'half-filled' double behind the thin plasterboard walls. Who knows what started it this morning? Some flatulence perhaps, a missile launched from the land of nod against enemy territory? *Direct hit, sir! She'll not recover from that blow!*

I can never understand what people are talking about in the morning. They talked last night before they went to bed, and absolutely nothing has happened in the meantime, so what can they be saying? These aren't the noises of people laughing about a ridiculous

dream one of them had; they are bickering about something, a baton of misery they picked up as soon as they woke up and which they will pass between each other throughout the day.

This argument certainly started off big, with both sides exchanging fire. Her voice now comes through the wall more clearly, but less regularly, whereas his emits a constant droning sound. It sounds as though a big fat bluebottle, about the size of a regulation football, is stuck in the wall space between our two rooms and every few seconds it roars into action trying to escape, beating its wings furiously, before wearing itself out and resting before another charge. These sorts of big rows usually end fairly quickly, in my experience. There is pure hatred in these exchanges, raw fury being launched from both sides.

Some rows grow gently from little seedlings of hate, most often when one partner has woken up in a bad mood and the other will not accept that there is no discernible reason for this. If there is anything guaranteed to put someone into a very bad mood it is being asked constantly why they are in a bad mood, when they don't even know themselves. It is a basic human right to be allowed to be grumpy every now and again and woe betide anyone who tries to take that away from someone or give it implied meaning.

'*Buzz buzz buzz?*'

'Nothing.'

'Buzz buzz buzz?'

'Nothing. Shut up.'

'Buzz? Buzz it me? It's me, buzzn't it?'

More silence.

'BUZZ BUZZ BUZZ! BUZZ BUZZITY BUZZ FUCKING BUZZ!'

'YES! ALRIGHT? Yes! NOW it is you! Fuck off and leave me alone you giant pain in the arse!'

Proof, if it were needed, that a problem shared is not, in fact, a problem halved, but a problem doubled: *one* of us had a problem, we have spoken about it … and now *two* of us have a problem! Two is always twice as big as one; it is a mathematical fact and I know that because I love maths. Maths is clean and constant, maths is reliable, maths has rules that allow us to work things out. Maths is a simple matter of right and wrong. Maths does not have moods. Two plus two will never wake up in a shitty mood and decide to be five just to upset all the other numbers. Nice and clean. Some numbers are better than others, obviously. Even numbers are better than odd, excepting multiples of five, which should be used whenever altering the volume control on a television. No television should ever have to suffer the ignominy of being left at volume thirteen. It makes me shudder just to think of it.

I do not subscribe to the view that it is best to talk about problems; like a fine whisky they should be bottled up and saved for later when they have had time to mature and develop. I might feel differently if I thought people discussed problems for the reason stated (in other words, to find a solution) but they don't really. What people really want when they talk about a problem is some sympathy. They want brows to be furrowed in front of them, and cooing noises to be made in their ear whilst their arms are stroked, because they have been led to believe that this is helpful, when really it isn't.

People on their own learn to deal with problems because they have to, in the same way that they learn to get rid of spiders because no one else is going to do it for them. You can scream and yell as much as you like but the spiders do not understand. It used to be that when I saw a spider in my bedroom I would go and sleep in another room ... until I saw a spider in there too. Living in a two-bedroom flat, there really aren't all that many options for relocation so my options were either to move to a mansion with six hundred bedrooms or learn to get rid of spiders. Fears and phobias are for those who can afford them, like fancy cars; the rest of us must get on with life.

I suppose Gemma could be good with spiders: she might have a no-nonsense, robust approach to all

things great and small, from insects, wasps and flies to Rottweilers and giraffes, crushing snails under her boots and drowning slugs in salt and Guinness. I would like to think I am comfortable enough with my masculinity not to feel somewhat undermined by having my spider extraction done by my girlfriend, but I think deep down I probably would. Would it be any better if she were an extreme arachnophobiac? In which case I could be spending the rest of my life walking ahead of her, clearing her path like a minesweeper, or getting up in the middle of the night to hold her hand when she needs to go and pee, guiding her gingerly to the loo just in case a tarantula is sitting at the bottom of the pedestal.

I would liken someone in a relationship discussing an external problem to a child whose excitement to run everywhere has led them to fall over. When young children fall over, there is a misconception that they start to cry immediately, but this isn't really the case. What happens first of all is a period of quiet assessment, where no pain exists but only the cold, hard facts.

I was standing upright and moving forward … and now I have a faceful of carpet. Hmm, how curious?

Most of the time, children left to their own devices will simply accept that this chain of events could not be understood by even the most advanced scientific minds and get up and continue with their play. However,

when a concerned parent is nearby and this thinking time is interrupted by cries of concern, the child will conclude that a problem beyond his comprehension has occurred and only then, when the pain has been validated by an adult, will they start to cry.

I must be in pain! If I cry now then I will get cuddled and kissed and given ice-cream.

Adults are really not so different.

Any second ... now? No.

Finally some silence from next door. A stalemate has been reached, and with it ends another period of time in which two people, supposedly in love, have done nothing but pick faults in one another:

You snore too much.

You fart in your sleep.

You make shit cups of tea.

You hate my mother.

You, you, *you!*

... And yet, curiously, when they eventually accept that their relationship has no future or, more to the point, one of them accepts the fact and the other is forced to go along with it (the true definition of breaking up by mutual agreement – 'she told me it was over and I agreed, eventually'), they will say earnestly to the other, whilst maintaining full eye-contact with head tilt and eyebrows raised in mock sympathy:

'It's not you, it's me.'

Who was it that first thought that this was a kinder way of telling someone that a relationship had no future? Of course I can see the logic, attempting as it does to sugar the pill by implying that *you* did nothing wrong and the end of our relationship is purely down to *me*.

'I am a fool to myself, I don't deserve love, blah blah blah … now get out and come back for your shitty stuff when I'm not here.'

Well, it doesn't help. Especially not if the 'you' in question is still madly in love with the 'me'. I can change me, tell me that I'm the problem for God's sake, tell me exactly what it is about me and I will do what I can to change … but to change you? I can't. Word it how you will, but what you always mean is 'I don't love you any more and you can cry as much as you like but there isn't a thing you can do to change the fact.'

The temptation here is to believe that this is some-how a uniquely British trait, slaves to our manners as we are, but I suspect it is more global. Most people begin a complaint with, 'I'm sorry but …' or they point out that someone is in the way with a very polite, 'Sorry, could I just squeeze past you there?' when what they really mean is, 'Get out of the aisle of the train you lardy piece of shit!' People always think they are helping by shifting blame and playing down problems but in truth the fairer way of dealing with things is to point out

exactly what someone has done wrong and give them a chance of finding happiness elsewhere by correcting themselves and finding someone else.

How is a man who burps the words 'I love you' and thinks that body odour is attractive to women ever going to improve himself if he is constantly told that he has done nothing wrong? It would be much better for Barbie to say, 'Listen Ken, it's not me, it's you. You stink.'

The whole relationship game is riddled with lies and half-truths and I don't regret leaving it behind at all. Much.

But on the upside, the *'fuck-you'*s and the *'you-always-do-this'*es from next door help to remind me of why I live the way I do and leave me with an (admittedly unpleasant) self-satisfied grin on my face. This is what they would have waiting for me, the people who sneer at me as I eat my dinners alone, the friends and colleagues who pry into my social life to see if they can't enliven their own stagnant relationships by seeking to set me up with one of their plucky, ever-cheerful friends who 'just hasn't met the right one yet'. They never tell you the truth about the person they want you to meet, but like car-sales people and estate agents they give you a potted history of all the best parts without warning you of the dry rot, the damage beneath the surface that is apt to come to the surface once the warranty period is over. Equally I can be sure that I have been misrepresented on the other side, so at least we can both spend our dinner in disappointed silence without one party feeling more aggrieved than the other.

Oh, he told you I was handsome did he? Ah, well I can only apologise. If I'm honest, I look roughly like this, most of the time, in fact this is me making an effort!

But once again, honesty is rejected as the best policy and replaced with play-acting and pointless platitudes. No one is honest with someone they find attractive because you would much rather someone loved a character being played by you, than for them not to love the real you.

And so back to Gemma, beautiful but increasingly forgetful of my existence Gemma.

When I hear the couple next door arguing, the voices I hear are mine and hers, ten years down the line. The question is whether I am being unduly negative or whether or not I am preparing for the inevitable. Of course I yearn to roll over in my bed and meet the eyes of someone whose beauty makes everything else in the world seem insignificant and have them smile back at me. I'd love to win the lottery too, but I don't bother buying a ticket any more because the odds seem stacked too heavily against me. Of course I might win a tenner every now and again, but who wants to spend the rest of their life living off the interest from ten pounds?

Staying single is simply a matter of playing the odds. In all my life, including my family, friends, the families of my friends and so on, I would say that I am aware of one couple who have been together all their lives and who I am almost certain are happier for it. Just one. The rest consists of relationships which have not yet had the chance to fail, couples who have stayed together against their will through obligation or responsibility or those who consider the back and forth of rowing and making up to be a sign of a passionate relationship. I would think that if you cannot get along with the person you live with at least *most* of the time, then there is probably some sort of problem.

My moods are down to me. When I am upset, it is because of something I have done and I can trace its origins back as far as I need to and then deal with it however I deem appropriate. When I need fresh air, I go out. When I need to get drunk, I drink. When I need a hug, I man up! Or else I wear a T-shirt that is slightly too small for me – the effect is the same. It certainly puts the musclemen I see in my gym, parading up and down in front of the mirror, into place when you consider that the real reason they are bursting out of their vests may simply be because they are imagining it is their mother's arms around them.

Dependence on others is a weakness, plain and simple. This military outlook has become a defence mechanism, a necessary response to a world that is constantly telling me that I am wrong in the way I choose to live my life. Sitcom and film storylines revolve around people my age looking for love, two-for-one offers in shops encourage family-size consumption and governments offer tax breaks to people who marry and have children (despite the fact that people in relationships already get everything half price). The tax breaks should be given to people like me, so that we can buy more DVDs and bottles of wine and forget our problems for two hours a night.

Being happy and single would be a lot easier if more people were willing to give it a try. My neighbours next-door are proof that, for some ridiculous reason, people would rather be locked into a miserable relationship than contemplate not being in one at all. What a depressing assessment of society that the only way to get through it is to drag someone else down with you! I believe passionately in love, I even believe in 'the one' to a certain extent, but I am willing to play the waiting game and patiently await their arrival rather than dive into relationships I know not to be right in the meantime.

Any second … now? Now?

And after a number of failed guesses, the alarm finally bursts into action and I reach back over my head

and turn it off. That was close enough, I reckon! Maybe today is going to be a good day after all, though if it is I certainly need to get my mind off the path it seems to be on at the moment. *I am* happy with the choices I have made. It seems even my sleeping brain seeks to remind me of the benefits of such a solitary lifestyle and this morning, as every morning, I have woken up in the familiar position of lying diagonally across the bed, making a Z shape with its top and bottom.

Look at this! You couldn't sleep like this if you had a girlfriend … Not without being kicked in the ribs every half an hour!

As true as this may be, the 45-degree angle is not one I am comfortable with and so I will right myself when I can shake my hangover enough to muster the energy to move. I have always believed that there is a reason they call it the right angle, and that is because the other 359 are all wrong. Although in truth, 356 would be more accurate as I have no beef with 180, 270 or the full 360 degrees.

The evidence of my love is that the 45-degree angle that exists between the bed frame and myself is the only one in the room; I got rid of all the others yesterday so that everything else is a picture of perfect symmetry. The bed sits underneath a cupboard from which hangs on either side a built-in wardrobe. Such large units are no longer fashionable but I cannot

escape my affection for their symmetry and sheer prac-
ticality. A unit this size can hide a multitude of sins in
a way that shelves and bookcases simply cannot.

Directly ahead of me, sitting in the space in front of
a bay window, is a desk upon which sits my list for the
day, a small kettle next to a basket containing two
sachets of coffee, two teabags and four sugars, a book
of 'house-rules' dressed up as a guest guide to the area
and a small television that in the digital age seems to go
back three miles from the screen. I wonder if I used
both the teabags whether she would be angry at my
greed? Over the right shoulder of the bed is the door to
the landing and mirrored on the left is the door to a
small en-suite bathroom.

I need my bedrooms to be ordered to allow me to feel
some shred of comfort in the morning. If my waking
eyes looked out over a mess of dirty clothes, wonky
pictures and dirty glasses I don't think I could resist the
to urge to pull the blanket over my head and bury my
face into it praying for some higher power I don't
believe in to step in and make it all go away. Once, in a
rather more posh hotel than this one, I stayed in a four-
poster bed. I found that the closed drapes around the
edge limited even further the damage to which morning eyes are subjected. There is always so much to cope
with on top of the mattress first thing in morning that
planning beyond it can seem too daunting a task.

I have resisted the urge to buy a similar bed for my home as I imagine that, eventually, sleeping alone in such a regal bed might feel even lonelier than it does in a standard double. I resent the fact that I have been made to feel that sleeping alone in a double bed is some kind of failure on my part. I would happily have a single bed but for the mockery that would ensue when I had visitors.

It is a source of confusion to me that as a child, say, in your first fifteen years, you learn more than you will ever learn in the same time period for the rest of your life. You learn how to walk and to talk, you learn about illness, death and about not getting your own way. You learn that life is sometimes unfair and that, for no reason at all, bad things happen to good people. You learn that there will come a time when all help ceases and you will be in sole charge of your own happiness and responsible for your own actions. You learn about money and what it is to be without it and you learn (if you are lucky) to ask questions about religion and what might exist beyond the world we know.

Not only this, but you must also get to grips with school, exams, bullying, physical education and physical attraction and the prospect of being poorly suited to success in both, not to mention the constant see-sawing of emotion caused by the hormonal changes going on

in your body and doubts about sexuality and the consequences this might have on your future.

All of these issues are to be confronted night after night, staring up at the ceiling on your own with your brain fit to burst, in a single bed. Then suddenly you become 'an adult' and you are told that the inability to find someone with whom you can share a double bed is the single biggest failure you can make in life. Well, bullshit! If I could, I would still have a neat and tidy little single bed while I am single … in fact if I am to be truly honest with you, and I don't see why I should stop now, I would have a cabin bed.

If you have the option available to you, I urge you to go and find your nearest furniture catalogue and spend a few minutes eyeing up the wide range of functional and stylish beds available for thc under-tens. Why it is only children who are granted the organisational joy of having a bed that sits high off the ground and also serves as a wardrobe, a desk and a secret den is beyond me. I still buy Variety Packs of cereal though – you can't take that joy away from me!

Before I step out from the plain, foot-high double bed that is my reality this morning, I must prepare my mind for the first tasks of the day. I must psyche myself up to get dressed without falling over, stubbing my toe or opening the wardrobe door into my face. Since getting dressed is the first thing I will do today it will therefore

set the standard for how the rest of the day is likely to progress.

Sometimes life sends you a warning that things are stacked against you and if I start with a failure in such a rudimentary task then I suppose I might just as well go straight back to bed for all the good the day will do. Like falling over at the beginning of a hundred-metre sprint, victory is all but impossible.

My desire to control everything that goes on inside my bedroom is a direct result of my inability to cope with everything that lurks outside it – not just this village, or Swindon when I am at home, but what lies beyond in the big, wide world. A thin pane of glass is a flimsy barrier between the world and myself, but it will just about hold strong until I fully open the blinds. The control for the slats is broken, so as I lie in bed staring at the window I can see that they are not closed tightly together. There is no light outside to penetrate the darkness in the room anyway.

The sun is already up but is hidden behind a blanket of thick cloud. The fine rain from last night has worsened, but only slightly. The skies are grey and it is as if all the colours have been washed away from the world by persistent rain. The greens of the trees and the blues of the skies are exposed as a veneer that couldn't stand-up to the abuse the world has given them.

Unlike most people, I love days like these!

114

Sunny days are arrogant – they appear to challenge you to try and achieve enough to warrant the splendorous conditions they have created for you. They exist for *mor*ning people to get out and steal all the achievement so that they can be back in bed by seven o'clock in the evening with smug grins on their faces and their freshly ironed pyjamas on their peachy skinned bodies.

'*Still in bed, Jon?*' these days cry. '*Why you've already wasted so much time! Go! Find your true love, feed them cherries on a chequered blanket by a lake. Ride bikes down hills and laugh heartily at the wonder of it all!*'

I'm alright, thanks. You keep that.

But there is no such challenge on a day like today. On a day when even the world outside the window cannot bring itself to smile, simply getting round to making a piece of toast feels like a victory over the circumstances.

The imaginary metronome in my head is running and I am counting down the last few seconds before I step out of bed out loud: a loud, clear tock to match every verbal tick. Tick. Tock.

My final thought is to wonder why, if my waking mind is so sure that I can be happy on my own, have I once again woken up lying on my side squeezing a pillow so tightly to my chest? Was I dreaming of Gemma? I am not even out of bed and already the world is too confusing to cope with. Like every day since 'the

number incident' I don't know whether to take heed of these unspoken signs that I need someone in my life, or whether to go on listening to the bickering and door slamming next door, and convince myself that they are the ones who have it wrong. I can't bear the thought that it might be like this for ever, because I know that as each year passes these arguments get harder and harder to remember. I meant them vividly eight years ago when I formed them, when the last person I loved told me that the fight was over.

Tick. Tock. Eight o'clock. Up and at 'em!

08.00

GET DRESSED

What to wear is a big concern to a lot of people. I am not predisposed to caring much for fashion. It annoys me that once something becomes fashionable, it becomes popular, but then in becoming popular, ceases to be considered fashionable any more. Large cities are teeming with people who, having run out of new clothes to wear or new ways to wear cloth of any sort, are on the lookout for household objects to wear. Ring-binders for hats and epaulettes made of spatulas are going to be big this summer, mark my words.

(Note: If on reading those words, you were at all tempted to check the year of publication and wonder if that might be actual fashion advice, then there is a number you should call – you have a problem.)

I, on the other hand, consider clothes to be some-thing I wear in order not to get thrown out of supermar-kets. Exposing one's penis by the courgettes is considered bad etiquette, and so trousers are required by the modern gentleman if he is not to be considered a mad genitalman. I do not so much wear clothing as allow it, against its will, to be wrapped around my angular body, giving me the appearance of someone wearing clothes handed down to him by an older brother regardless of my age.

People who are into fashion notice these problems straight away and take pity on me. They would no sooner point out that what I am wearing looks terrible than point at a cancer sufferer who has lost their hair; after all it isn't my fault, just a problem from which I suffer. Heaven forbid they might make a suggestion as to how I could look better in clothes, but just give me enough Jean-Paul Gaultier-designed Egyptian silk rope with which to hang myself. I know people notice these things because one former girlfriend let slip the secret pity of the fashionistas over a coffee once we had 'become friends' following our break-up.

'Oh, I'll never forget the first time we met,' she giggled, preparing me for an anecdote about a particular witty riposte I had made or how our eyes connected and she fell in love in a way she had never thought previously possible. 'You were wearing those fucking awful jeans with those ghastly black and white trainers! Where did your arse used to go in those jeans. Urgh!'

Charming. I never did remember what she was wearing, which I like to think wasn't a lack of care for her,

but a prioritisation of more important things. It was enough that we were making eye contact or that she laughed at my jokes. I would no sooner judge a person by the clothes they were wearing than I would judge a car by the scent of the air freshener hanging from the rear-view mirror.

Since I will be spending today in the car I do not have to make any attempt to look presentable so I remove from my suitcase a pair of Wallace and Gromit boxer shorts I have owned for at least a decade, some jeans and a plain black T-shirt. I buy new clothes with the same regularity as when I buy a new car, namely, when the old one has ceased to work. When my undergarments no longer conceal my possessions, or when my waistline exceeds their elastic capabilities, they get replaced, but not a moment before.

I can only hope Gemma is not the sort of girl to judge a man on his sartorial elegance or else this is another bridge we are going have to cross together. In my stronger mind I want to believe that if she does judge a man by his clothing then she isn't the girl for me, but in truth I am so desperate to finally be with someone that if she looked at what I was wearing and had to stifle a tut of disgust, I would be crushed.

08.16

HAVE BREAKFAST

Some mornings I like to switch on the news straight away to find out if anything exciting has happened overnight, but recently I find I can't face it without first having had a strong cup of tea. Such a British reaction to things, I know, and I think in truth it is the time spent staring out of the window holding something warm that I crave. Watching the news is like being given a huge 'To do' list for the entire world. I can barely cope with my own, and it doesn't have things on it like:

1. Diffuse tensions in Middle East
2. Prevent all murders (solve existing cases where needed)
3. Combat global warming (or spend months in prehab, reverting intelligence back far enough to successfully enter 'Clarksonian denial')
4. Generate more nurses and teachers and policemen (How?)

5. Solve the UK's ongoing international financial crisis and what to do about the bankers
6. Break for elevenses – prepare list for afternoon

Everything outside is already so grey and desperate with a vague foreboding that I don't need to overload myself with the specifics of what horrors are waiting for me beyond my current horizon, sure to leap out at me when I step out of the front door and turn to face the world. If I don't check the news I can convince myself for a few brief moments that everything outside has disappeared and I am the last survivor on earth. Although this seems pleasant at first, no fantasy can thrive in my mind for too long before the negative voice kicks in with a fatal dose of realism.

You don't have any practical skills. You'll die as soon as all the fresh vegetables run out, if they haven't been wiped out already by whatever killed all the people. Besides, you'll get even lonelier.

It is certainly true that there is a huge difference between knowing that people are out there and choosing to avoid them (as is my current position) and wanting to speak to someone but knowing that there is nobody there. This is the cause of my irrational hatred of those people who say things like, 'I often find I can be loneliest in a crowded room!'

Oh, fucking can you? Well, that's a huge coincidence, because I often find I can be hungriest just after I've eaten a massive cake.

Most people who say things like this have simply never had to confront a situation in which they want for all the world to talk to someone but have literally not a single option available to them for conversation. Please do not confuse loneliness with disliking your friends or, rather more likely, the friends of your friends. It amazes me how often the people who love the people we love can seem so abhorrent to us. Whatever slight issue you may have with your friends, you can be sure they will be amplified one hundred times over when you see your friends once removed.

If your best friend Sarah can be a tad gregarious, then you can be sure that Sarah's parties will be filled with screaming, obnoxious morons. Similarly, if old buddy Michael can be a little dull, then expect his gathering to have all the joy of a beloved pet's funeral (on the moon). This is why everybody gets drunk at parties and then, when drunk, ends up sleeping with one of the people who drove you to drinking in the first place. Now you have become one of them! All you have to do is make sure you are drunk all the time you spend together and they will always seem worth sleeping with; it's not such a heavy price to pay, is it? Downstairs at breakfast I will no doubt be forced to sit alongside

couples who find themselves stuck with the person they settled for one night forty or so years ago. Now they have weekends away, not from the area they live in, but the lives they have ended up with.

I am not looking forward to dining with strangers downstairs, nor to the pot of tea that will be presented to me when I sit down. I like tea in a mug and can never get the balance of milk and sugar quite right in a cup and saucer. At home I have a routine – there are rules! Some hot water goes in first to warm the mug, then is tipped out before milk and tea bag go in together with one sugar and fill to the top. Leave for a minute, stir thoroughly, then drink. Some people get very angry about my putting the milk in with the tea bag before the water, but a scientist once told me that the resulting liquid then forms an emulsion rather than a mixture, which coats the tongue more evenly with flavour.

I won't lie – I can't taste any difference. But it pleases me to know that there is a scientific basis for my actions. Where such evidence exists it should certainly be put to use. As long as you don't tell people you can't taste the difference, people still tend to shut up pretty quickly when you explain why you do as you do in so much detail. Probably just out of pity for me at the way I live my life, but never mind, a win is a win.

Since it is a Sunday and I will not have to cook any of it myself, nor wash up afterwards, I will treat myself to

a full fry-up at Mrs Snooty's expense. While I say this is also a treat, it is also a form of exercise for me, a continuation of my training programme aimed at the perfection consumption of one of Britain's best loved meals. When eating a fry-up finally gets acknowledged as an Olympic sport, I will surely be our Steve Redgrave. A people's favourite, strong and consistent, competing in a sport that actually nobody is all that sure about, but for the fact we seem to do quite well at it.

Creaking down the stairs I can hear a low murmur of conversation being pierced at irregular intervals by the cold, harsh clinking of cutlery against china. This is always the moment I think about turning back and eating something on the road in my car, for fear of the moment when I walk through the door and a room full of faces stare up at me as I enter. I know they are just guests here as I am, yet they manage to make me feel as though I am interrupting a special family meal. Will I have to wait to be seated or do I simply grab a table? I am somewhat particular about where I sit to eat; ideally I would like to be tucked in a corner somewhere looking out at the room. This is either cowardice or else I had secret ninja training when I was a child that I have since forgotten about.

As I enter, I make eye contact with nobody. To my left there is a table with cereals and juice and a door leading to the kitchen, from which emanates a warm

egg-scented air, with a sizzle of bacon and the faint sound of an old radio playing new music. Nobody comes through to seat me so I pick a seat at a table made for one (presumably for me, though in my paranoia I imagine she only cleared the second place setting once others had already been seated. 'He booked for two, but he's on his own ... I know, the cheek of it!').

At once I am struck by the gaping chasm between my life and the film version of it playing in my head. In the film version I am sitting in a small, boutique-style coffee house which serves breakfast but does it in an ironic way.

Can you believe it? Beans! From a tin! If it were any more random it would be uniform. Right?

In the film I would slowly fall in love with the French waitress who brings me my coffee but who always seems to have a tear forming in her eye because she longs to make a career from the paintings she works on in the evenings. But this is not a film. Here, in the unedited, straight to DVD version that is my life, my order is being taken by a sour-faced, thrice-divorced mother of four who wishes I were anywhere in the world but here. She takes the order and heads back into the kitchen, leaving behind a silver rod with a stand at one end and a brown-sauce-stained piece of card with the number six clipped on to the other.

With the acceptance of the truth of my situation comes a far more painful, real memory of a chance I had to avoid the eight years of solitude that have just drained by. The girl who didn't join in with the chattering in the hotel I worked at, serving breakfasts when I was twenty-one – Rita – a small and heartbreakingly beautiful Spanish girl who tended to the dishwasher and made round after round of toast.

She, like me, worked silently in the corner and there were moments I can remember as clearly as if they happened yesterday in which we would exchange a knowing smile across the room as one of the older ladies shrieked her dismay at how greedily the sausages were being snaffled up from her buffet. Rita is typical of many girls who got away, the ones I call the 'near mrs', but in truth the near miss was theirs, not mine.

Eight years on I still wonder if I saw someone I liked in here now, whether or not I would have the courage to do anything about it. Back then there seemed to be a world of opportunity before me, so I suppose it didn't seem as important as it does now to engage with everyone I like. Now I realise how rarely those situations arise, but that only means the pressure and implied importance of each one would get the better of me.

But I'm forgetting Gemma. My chance has come around at last, like thinking that you have missed your bus only to find that it was running late. Not that I'm

comparing Gemma to a bus, and certainly not the back of one. Although maybe the bus will turn out to be full, or as it gets closer I will see that the sign above the driver reads 'Sorry – Not In Service'. I can't fall into the trap of thinking that Gemma is the answer to my problems because I know that just because you wait eight years to like someone does not mean that they will necessarily feel the same way when you do. Besides which, having been single for eight years I can tell you that girls simply find such a long period on the sidelines a little weird. A couple of years lying fallow after the breakdown of a relationship implies that you committed properly to the last one and needed some time to regain yourself after its end, but eight years suggests some time spent at Her Majesty's pleasure after a horrific incident which ended the last one.

I can't ever believe that the girls I like could be attracted to me and, even if I could, and if they had been, all I see is an inevitable descent from a perfect beginning into the hatred and disappointment with which all relationships must surely end. I don't know if this is right, but sitting down at my table I am trying to stop the dark thoughts and focus back on the here and now. Have I just cheated on Gemma already by thinking back to how things might have been with Rita? If it is true that there is 'the one' for all of us, could it be that I missed mine?

From my seat, I look down upon four items on the table: the silver pole with a card held in place at the top displaying my table number (six), a fake purple flower in a small blue vase and salt and pepper shakers. I am finding it almost impossible to position these items satisfactorily on the round table on which I now find myself. They have to go somewhere in the middle, obviously, or things will be all lopsided, but where? If I can't look at the table without being distracted then I am never going to be able to get through breakfast comfortably.

I can put the salt and pepper either side of the flower in the centre of the table, but then I don't know what to do with the silver spike. I could just put it on the floor, but I would know it was there, laughing at me while I was eating my food. That would be no worse a sign of defeat than painting over the sides of a Rubik's Cube. Out of sight, out of mind is something lazy people say to pardon themselves from having to tidy up. If it genuinely worked as a philosophy then adults would continue to close their eyes, put their fingers in their ears and sing 'la la la!' at the top of their voices whenever they felt intimidated.

Things have to be faced up to eventually and so this situation will have to be resolved and the number will have to go somewhere. If I remove it from its base it will lie flat and I can deal with the base later. The

problem then is the writing – which way should it face? And will it still be visible when my breakfast is ready?

The longer this puzzle goes unsolved, the more the noise coming from the other tables is starting to annoy me. As hard as I try to concentrate on the important matter in hand, fragments of the tedious conversations of strangers bounce off the walls and the ceiling and ricochet into my brain, invading my headspace. I can hear two old ladies who seem to be discussing the recent death of a third. I do pity them that they are already having to talk of such things at breakfast, but somehow I don't get the impression they are upset as they seem keen to portray.

'It's Peter I feel sorry for – they were inseparable.'

Then there are groans of agreement. Their grief doesn't seem genuine. It strikes me that the commiserations and the 'woe-is-me's are really there simply so that they don't feel guilty about being glad just to have something to talk about. How long will this enforced period of politeness about the recently deceased hold strong before they can both be honest about what they always thought about Old Lottie? It is so much easier to grieve for the dead than to care for the living. At least in death we are all perfect.

'When did it get like this, eh? We used to go to parties and weddings, now it seems it's just funerals.'

Perhaps I am being too harsh. This soulless breakfast room in the middle of somewhere is no place for two women to be facing up to their own mortality and the realisation that things only will only get worse for them as they grow ever older. I know this time of life will come to me and if I am not careful I will have wasted my youth on mornings like these. I will make a conscious effort to kick a ball across a field the next time I get a chance, or something equally spritely.

I can also hear three businessmen, much younger and more confident voices than those of the old ladies. I can hear them mainly because they want me to hear them; me and everyone else in the area. I doubt there is anyone in a twenty-mile radius who really gives a shit about the consequences for DIM Logistics of the new figures from Japan and yet we are being subjected to them anyway. The volume of their conversation is designed to show their importance, but they are kidding themselves if they think any significant business deal has ever been brokered over beans and runny eggs in a bed and breakfast hotel. I think that even the men discussing the figures know deep down that they are of no importance whatsoever, but they are also aware that if they acknowledged that to themselves they would have no reason to get out of bed in the morning. We all have to constantly repress the idea that there is no point to our lives and these men are no

different, just a lot louder and with a lot more gel in their hair.

I am definitely getting distracted. Concentrate, Jon! If I stood the order number up, facing me, I could line up the other items in front of it with the flower in the middle. This is undoubtedly the best option, but still not perfect as, although the view from my seat is fine, the view from above would reveal the table to be unsymmetrical.

My skin starts to tingle with the frustration of it all and so I take a deep breath and move up to a higher level of concentration to prevent myself from screaming and kicking the table over. There is a simple solution if I could just be allowed to concentrate for a moment. I remind myself that this *is* important. If I can't even get something simple like this right, then how can I possibly begin to deal with everything else the world will throw at me today?

Another elderly couple are having an impassioned debate in what sounds to me like Turkish. I think it must be about something very important, but that's probably just the effect of the foreign accents. They seem to care so much, flailing arms and furrowed brows on both sides. At one point the man reaches over and encloses the woman's hands inside his; a powerful passive-aggressive gesture. I imagine it makes her feel claustrophobic and unable to escape but seems to show

such love and affection. Without thinking I extend all the fingers and thumbs on my hands, just to prove to myself that I can.

There is a Freudian theory that men are inherently attracted to waitresses and barmaids because they serve hot foods and beverages like your mummy used to when you were a child. If this is the case, then my breakfast order is delivered by a mummy who clearly thinks I am a total prick. She slams down a plate of food and takes the number away without saying a word.

Not to worry, the removal of the number has won her affections quite enough for me. Lined up across the centre of the table in a neat line are now salt, flower and pepper. Perfect! Back on track.

Eating out can be a source of incredible stress for the more fastidious amongst us. I have been so upset by things like grammatical inconsistency in the past that I have chosen to eat elsewhere. I can tell you that most other people don't see the errant use of apostrophes as a valid reason not to eat somewhere. It's not that the mistake itself is that important – I'm not a fool enough to believe that someone's ability to spell is connected to their ability to cook – but it shows an unwillingness to ask for help.

A conversation flashes in my mind. It took place towards the end of my last relationship, over a particularly gruelling cooked breakfast designed to clear the

air after another Saturday-night drunken argument. In an attempt to lighten the mood on entry I commented, 'Look! They've put an apostrophe on the beans', pointing to the board behind the counter. 'Bean *is* on toast … stingy portions!'

'Well, we've got to eat fucking somewhere!' came the reply.

Another comic misfire, that joke detonating somewhere over the road in Boots. It wasn't meant as a criticism really, just a manifestation of the fact that I cared for her so much that it was no effort at all to try and make sure that everything around us was perfect. My hunting around for ideal restaurants, my careful seat locating at the cinema, my planning our evenings so far in advance; everything had a purpose, everything was designed to make our time together more pleasant by reducing the risk of unwelcome neighbours, bad food, rushed service and the myriad other things which, although they might not make or break an evening, could serve to take the gloss off the memory.

Life has quite enough unpleasantness in store for all of us without taking risks with that which could easily be controlled. Perhaps I missed the point, which was that we should simply have been glad to be together whatever our surroundings, and that actually the more challenging the situation, the greater the test of our relationship's ability to withstand heavy weather.

I believe there are two types of people in this world: 'Putters' and 'Leavers'. You can find out which one you are by how you respond to a question such as, 'Where are your keys?' If you pat your left front trouser pocket, realise they are not there and then point to a hanger, bowl or table and say the words, 'They're there, where I *put* them', then you are a putter.

Congratulations! Putters are people who think about all their actions and are annoyed by losing things, which they consider to be a failure on their part and not simply something that happens from time to time.

If, on the other hand, you respond by raising your eyebrows, shrugging your shoulders and crying, 'I don't know! Wherever I left them!', then you are a leaver.

Oh dear.

Leavers flit through their lives dropping and losing items they profess to care about because chasing down something shiny or going to stroke a dog was more important to them than looking after their keys. As much as I hate these people, I cannot help but enjoy their affection for life and confess to being attracted, in the main, to people who live differently to me.

It is the case in most relationships that one partner will be classified as a putter, with the other being a leaver. This is simply because a partnership of two putters will result in the murder of one by the other over an argument about which direction the tins in the

cupboard should face. A coalition of leavers will result in both parties dying of dysentery. And so the rules dictate that a leaver will ensnare a putter, who will chase them around from one furious passion to another, picking up things that were knocked over and shutting doors and locking them behind.

My last girlfriend and I fell firmly into this category, she wanted me to help her be less impulsive and I wanted her to help me enjoy my life more and worry less. Sadly, opposites, while they may attract, cannot be maintained and we grew to hate each other.

Looking back now, years later, I can't believe she ever let me touch her to begin with. When I think about it now – the thought of my bony, white body pressed up against hers, and of her having to tolerate my wet breath against her neck – it's a wonder to me that she was never sick into my face. In truth I have never had a relationship that lasted any more than two years before all excitement faded away completely and all that was left was routine.

Could it be different this time? She might be fed up with me after two weeks, let alone two years, and whatever peace of mind I have built up for myself over the last eight years would be shattered. She might of course turn out to be even more of a putter than me, and cling to our relationship with such tenacity and ferocity that I will become a Born Again Leaver.

Loving someone is very different to staying with them because at least you don't hate them. By the end of two years you probably know most of what there is to know about who you are with, certainly all of what they want you to know about them, so that all you can do is grow more annoyed by the things that bother you. What started as an amusing slurping sound your partner makes when they drink from a bottle, a quirk of their personality that makes them the person you love, will eventually be nothing more than a disgusting, gutteral punch to your solar plexus every time you see them even reach for a drink.

Watching her grow less happy around me was devastating. At first, she just got bored of what I was and questions I asked became rhetorical, but slowly that indifference turned to frustration and hate. You can't see when someone is happy – there isn't an outward sign with humans like there is with sexual arousal or a dog's wagging tail.

However hard it may be to spot, you can certainly see when it has gone missing though. Some argue that perfection occurs at the point when there is nothing left to take away, and perhaps it is true that happiness occurs simply as a result of a lack of unhappiness.

In my case, I always seem to be able to find something else to complain about, some other small imperfection to fuss over. My fastidious attention to detail,

which can be amusing in the beginning, eventually becomes grating and sooner or later creates an atmosphere where my intolerance of failure is so claustrophobic that no single event can bring any joy.

Cooked breakfasts are a perfect case in point.

When we first got together my girlfriend (along with my friends) took great pleasure in watching the way I would eat, eyes transfixed and grins wide. My goal when eating any meal is at first to identify the nicest parts of that meal, and push them aside to eat at the end. Many people will grab instantly for their knife and fork and begin shovelling inconsistent mouthfuls of food into their greedy faces, but that serves only to deny themselves the pleasure of the logistical phase!

Ordering my mouthfuls gives me a process, an incentive to get through the meal, a reward for finishing, and ensures that my final memory, in this case of breakfast, is of triumphantly lifting a forkful of perfection into my mouth before folding my napkin neatly underneath my fork and knife which are placed together in the centre of a cleaned plate.

This can be done with most meals, except for those which offer no variation – the boring foods – porridge, soup, cereal and so on. Bowls full of indeterminate slop

138

to be ingested until full. Where a plate has different elements, job number one is to identify 'the headliner'.

The headliner is the best part of the show, the main attraction, and as such must take their place at the top of the bill. I would no sooner begin eating a chicken jalfrezi by eating all the pieces of chicken than I would programme a festival with 'Derek Mickleton and his Mystical Mouth Organ' headlining over the Gipsy Kings. Don't like the Gipsy Kings? Fine, screw you! Don't come to my festival.

With a cooked breakfast, there is no real 'headline event'; much like a Sunday roast the end goal here is a forkful with a piece of everything, and a scrap of toast/ Yorkshire pudding to run around the plate soaking up the overspill. We can consider the best elements to be:

The fat juicy middle of the sausage, the meaty end of the rasher of bacon, the yolk of the egg, the central part of the tomato (away from the stalk), the crispier end of the hash brown (occurring at the end containing the smaller of the two acute angles where, for the sake of argument, we consider the hash brown to be a right-angled triangle). This is all allowing for variations according to personal preference and constituent elements, obviously.

As such, the first task after placement of the break-fast and following the planning phase is to eliminate

the weaker elements, the egg white, the sausage ends, the fatty part of the bacon, excess bean and tomato. This can be done in almost any order, though I advise the pairing of bacon and tomato takes preference, with sausage and egg also working well. When this is done, I often find it is time for a break. Time to lean back and do a bit of further admin before moving on to the climactic finale!

Questions to ask here include:

* Am I sure that I have left only the best parts of the breakfast?
* Am I likely to run out of anything or will there be a surplus? This needs to be dealt with immediately.
* How many mouthfuls am I likely to get out of what remains?

This last question should be what guides you from here to completion. Obviously, an egg yolk can be split into no more than four quarters to be a worthy constituent of a mouthful, so we are looking at four final forkfuls. After cutting up four good pieces of bacon, sausage, hash brown and, should it be present, black pudding (how much of each is down to your personal taste), and allowing at least three beans per section, it is once again time to eliminate the remainder.

The next is my favourite part of the breakfast. Provided your technique has been efficient and the plate and its components are still warm, what you have now is four perfect piles of squishy goodness. As soon as you make your first incision into the yolk, it's a race against time to make sure it doesn't go cold or dribble out of its casing completely. As discussed, the expert will leave a corner of well-buttered toast to quickly mop up any liquids left on the plate, but this must be done quickly to become a constituent part of the final mouthful rather than a disappointing addendum.

Ending a meal on a bad mouthful will sully the memory of it entirely. No dinner can cope with its denouement involving the spitting of a mouthful of steak gristle into a napkin, a spoonful of curry with no meat but only rice and sauce, the few peas and carrots at the end of a roast dinner. I find a depressing comparison here to be drawn between dinners and relationships. Perhaps my ability to draw comparisons between women I have loved and cooked breakfasts is why I find myself single, but where the links exist I feel I should point them out.

At the beginning of a relationship there seems to be so much promise and excitement as each new discovery forms a stronger bond and all points to a perfect future together. There is a part of me that thinks this the perfect time to break up and go your separate ways.

Like a football manager who has taken a side from the bottom of the Conference to the Premier League, step away while you can still be idolised rather than staying until the bitter end, because bitter is all it will be in my humble experience.

That it should be newsworthy when an elderly couple celebrates a long wedding anniversary is evidence enough of how rare such an occurrence is, and we should not be fooled into thinking either that simply because they have stayed together for sixty years that they are happier than they would be if on their own.

Nobody likes change. Staying in a relationship beyond the honeymoon period, be it a literal honeymoon or not, is simply a trade-off. You are trading the irrational fear of dying alone for the constant ebb and flow of a life lived in compromise and without personal space. I am quite sure there will be those reading this who consider themselves to be in a relationship which allows them to express themselves fully, spend time on their own and also commit to another person's happiness.

Bully for you – feel free to write to me and I might change my mind – but I suspect that there are far more who are still looking for the right person. I suspect there are far more people who thought they had found the right person but discovered only that they were to feel the pain all the more acutely when something went

wrong, or they were taken away from them. The pain caused by these latter events is crippling. Anyone who tells you that it is better to have loved and lost than to have never loved at all has never done both.

Don't wait for the gristly end – measure your mouthfuls carefully.

I finish my breakfast, fold my napkin and place the knife and fork neatly together on top, but when I look over at the other side of the table, there is nobody there to smile back or applaud my completion. It's just me, feeling fat. No Spanish Rita, not even an equally hungover friend. The more elaborate the meal and the more perfect my execution, the greater my sense of shame at having eating it alone. This is worsened by the fact that I also inevitably seem to eat too much. I have once again reached a point where all I can do is make noise, in the hope that releasing sound will make space where currently there is none.

Bbbbuuuuueeeerrrrgggggghhhh!

It doesn't work, and the fact that when I attempt to sit forward my distended belly pushes me back and holds me captive on my chair like a greedy turtle on its back makes me hate myself even more.

You big, fat, greedy, little wanker! You could have eaten half of that, and given the other half to someone who might have enjoyed it just as much as you, and might love you for having made it for them.

That is true enough. Sat high up in the Dales I once drank wine, grilled meat and ate fresh, vibrant salad looking across a beautiful sunset after a day spent at a place I hold very dear in my heart, after a particularly tranquil afternoon when everything seemed like it would be OK. It hurt me to think that no one would ever know the perfection of that moment but me, and I would never be able to describe it to them as I have been unable to express the beauty of that spot here in words.

Somehow, happiness is not diminished by being shared out with other people. It thrives like bacteria, duplicating itself for as many people as want to be infected by it. The happier you manage to make yourself on your own, the more acutely aware you become of the futility of it.

As miserable as the end of a relationship can be, it is the absence of a deeper happiness when alone that overrides most of what I have just written. Looking over the table and not seeing a smiling face, having no one to plan things for or buy gifts for commits me to a half life. It is my desire to share perfection, not half my miseries that makes me text Gemma. Reaching for my phone I begin to compose a message:

144

HAVE BREAKFAST

Hi Gemma. Sorry it has taken me so
long to reply, I'm simply a moron. It
would be great to see you some time,
let me know when is good for you. Jon

And before I can think twice about it, I press send.
Now you've gone and done it.

09.36

FIFTY THOUSAND ... AND FOUR

I came up from breakfast, scribbled a few notes down on a scrap of paper, showered and packed my things and paid the lady (who I noticed went straight upstairs afterwards to check what state I'd left her room in; she would have been almost disappointed to find I had made the bed and folded my used towels neatly on the bathroom floor). I loaded my car and filled up with petrol at the petrol station down the road from the guest house before heading out of town and on to the motorway.

I did all this and Gemma still hadn't fucking replied to my message.

It's a Sunday morning so chances are she is still asleep. Whether or not she is alone in her bed is a matter for my overactive and uniquely negative imagination. She isn't alone in what I'm imagining, and she isn't asleep either. Driving should clear my head – it did the trick with whatever was bothering me when I set off.

If she still hasn't replied by the time I get home then what will I do? I could call in at her work to see what she is doing; perhaps I will see her in the arms of another man and I can stop thinking that there might be any hope of a happy ending for us. Oddly, I think I almost want this to happen, as if seeing that would take the matter out of my hands. No pressure to be the right man for her any more, as she has chosen someone else. As any football fan will tell you, it's the hope that eventually kills you.

Despite all my best efforts to think about other things I cannot stop waiting for the message to beep into my life, which it stubbornly refuses to do. I glance down to check the time in the hope that I will discover that somehow I have entered a kind of black hole and that only three minutes have passed since I sent the initial text. Admittedly checking the clock in my car won't necessarily give me a fully accurate impression of the time, nor would checking my watch, nor indeed checking both. I keep my watch fast so I'm not late for pressing engagements (the logic being that if I think it's later than it actually is, I'll set off sooner than actually necessary).

This being such a fiendishly intelligent plan, I decided to keep all my clocks fast to stop me checking one clock against another, but set them all forward by differing amounts, so as not to grow complacent. If my watch is four minutes fast, but my hallway clock is two minutes

fast, my microwave clock seven minutes fast and my car display ten whole minutes fast, I will never truly know what the time is, only that by leaving when the clock in front of me tells me to leave, I am ahead of it. A selfless gesture on my part which ensures I am never late, but really only means that I spend time waiting not only for people who are late but also for people who are on time.

Obviously, if I kept all my clocks fast by exactly four minutes I would eventually grow so used to arriving four minutes early that I might be tempted to leave my house four minutes late, and then what? From there I would slide down the slippery slope descending through 'assuming the person I am meeting will be late', then down into 'setting off late deliberately to see if I can shave time off my Personal Best journey time' and eventually becoming the kind of person everybody assumes will be late. How these people are allowed to exist is beyond me; being late is always a status play. People who arrive late do so precisely because they know they will be waited for. Until we all make a decision to leave behind those who do not respect schedules, they will never learn. If this means leaving your twelve-year-old son in a service station on the M1 then so be it. He has to learn.

Glancing down to the clock on the dashboard, before I see the time my eyes are drawn to the milometer. It reads: 50 004 miles.

This is not good! While I had been thinking about Gemma and wondering why she hadn't texted me back, I had completely forgotten that I was nearing my next ten-thousand-milestone. There are two types of people in this world: people who take an inordinate amount of pleasure from seeing the exact moment that their car's mileage ticks over from a filthy mess of nines to any multiple of ten thousand miles, and people who are dead inside.

I remember having looked down when I arrived back after the gig yesterday and noticing that I had done 49 992 miles, making a mental note to keep an eye on it. Now that moment has passed me by, never to return. This is exactly the sort of careless mistake I pride myself on, nay I define myself, by *not* making.

Fucking fuck! I can feel my legs starting to tingle with frustration, I yearn to run or to lash out against something to make it feel like what just happened wasn't my own stupid fault. I know that this is not something that should affect me as badly as it seems to, but knowing that only makes it worse.

When, in the past, I have been down about my life for no justifiable reason, friends have thought it helpful to point out all the things that make me fortunate in an attempt to pacify my mood. In truth, this only ever makes it worse. I know very well that I have no reason to feel aggrieved – I am fully aware of how lucky I am,

but knowing it and still being down makes me hate myself all the more. Similarly here, the knowledge that the majority of people, even if they were frustrated by having missed the milestone, would simply tut or sigh and then move on makes me all the more irritated by the side of my personality which continues to pick away at myself.

50 004. *Urgh. 4. 4. 4.*

I pull off the motorway at the next service station, some three miles down the carriageway, to get my head together as I can feel the overwhelming urge to floor the accelerator and stop only when stopped by something bigger and heavier than me. Slowing to ten miles per hour and turning into a parking space (I am too angry to even think about reverse parking), in my desperation I begin to wonder if I reversed for seven miles whether the mileage would move backwards to exactly 50,000. I know deep down that this is unlikely but I am still too upset to let this one go. I have been looking forward to that figure since I witnessed the turn to 40,000 while driving a friend to a gig in the Midlands last Christmas. I remember telling him to lean over and watch but he wasn't bothered – he just carried on staring out of the window. People are seldom interested in the things I am. Fifty thousand is the second biggest milestone too, behind the big ton of course. Now there is nothing to look forward to.

It's not that these are life-alteringly significant moments – I'm not stupid enough to believe that – but I see them as little bonuses, the likes of which crop up every now and again in life to reward you for paying attention. The neatness of the number and the line of fat, little '0's is a pat on the back for all those people who understand that, as regularly as the hands of fate tear and scratch at your plans, they can reward you too. If I didn't take pleasure in the neatness and order that can shine through in the universe then I could never cope with the death and destruction it wreaks in equal measure.

The fact remains that if I had not been thinking of her, I would have seen the 50k. She is clouding my judgement. I wind down the windows of my car to feel the breeze against my face, close my eyes and start to take deep breaths, strangling the steering wheel with my clenched fists. Some quiet meditation and then a coffee is in order.

10.38

COFFEE BREAK[DOWN]

There is a place I like to go which makes the things I worry about seem insignificant. I would even go as far as to say that of all the places in which you could find me happiest (though I must point out that by finding me you have more than likely inflicted upon that happiness a fatal wound), an autumnal afternoon, sat quietly on a rock at the water's edge some half a mile upstream of a certain waterfall is hard to beat. Quite a specific place to suggest, I'll admit, though in truth it doesn't have to be any waterfall in particular; to me they all share the same energy and characteristics. I close my eyes and transport myself to the last time I was there in the hope that some of the tension I feel will disappear.

A perfect afternoon involves me arriving first at the body of the falls and staring for a long while into the white water as it crashes downwards, pounding the rocks below, before climbing up its side and walking away until all the drama and the deep noise from earlier begin to fade. I walk until all that remains as a clue to what lies ahead is a gentle murmuring; a kind of radio static which, rather than irritate, serves to emphasise the feeling of brief purgatory from something more sinister.

What excites me first and foremost about this spot is that were you to have approached from further upstream, as the water itself has done, now slipping by me in blissful ignorance, there is no way that you could predict what lies ahead. Knowing something that nothing around me knows gives me an undignified but nevertheless inherently human sense of superiority.

Although picturesque and quaint enough in summer, and far more popular with daytrippers, I prefer to visit in autumn when the grey skies above lend the water a darker and more ominous power and make its depth more difficult to decipher. Huge, jutting rocks break through at irregular intervals along its width, breaking up its otherwise regular flow and dominating the trickling waters.

At that moment, those rocks seem impenetrably strong, as though the water has no option but to yield to their weight and simply skirt around them, but over time they will be relentlessly eroded into submission. This slow and steady approach to achieving its goals is the first attribute that I find fascinating about flowing water. Such great things will be achieved and yet no single step will be visible to the naked eye. It is not just

the rocks that will disappear – the fall itself is working its way slowly backwards, eating up the scenery.

Eventually entire landscapes will be formed and re-formed by the relentless waters. In centuries to come, the spot on which I am sitting won't even exist, never mind the problems which occupy my mind as I sit here. I laugh to think that, if such things exist (and I doubt very much that they do), my ghost will appear to the onlookers of the future to be hovering in mid-air, looking out over seemingly nothing at all.

So many silent power struggles are going on here, and so much more lies ahead, but sitting on my rock, eating my lunch, it seems a scene of such calm tranquil-lity. Leaves and insects float gently across the still surface of the slower moving waters by my side. The sound the water makes as it trickles over the pebbles that have themselves been smoothed and perfected over time is a gentle sound – it licks at my eardrums. It isn't necessary to be immersed in water to feel cleansed by it.

In my mind, more inspiring still is the enthusiasm with which the water continues to surge forward, despite the futility of its cyclical journey. There will be no finish line for these tiny particles; there will be no winner. If they survive the drop that lies ahead and make it as far as the ocean, they will more than likely simply be picked up and dropped back on higher ground to start their journey all over again, with miles

and miles of new course to navigate and new obstacles to overcome. It cannot ever stop.

Sitting there on a slightly cold but not unpleasant afternoon helps me confirm that you do have to come away from people in order to think clearly about more important things. There on my rock I can take stock of where I am, how I have arrived here and where I am heading next – the bigger picture. To me, people are like the rocks that would break up the flow of the river. They burst into your life and impede your progress. There are relationships to maintain, bills to pay, there is work to do and fun to have before you can carry on with your journey.

A select few will leave the spot they are in when you arrive and travel along with you a part of the way. It may seem, for a while at least, that your trip is no longer one that need be made alone. But no sooner have you become accustomed to their company, then they will get caught up on something, flow down a different channel or just break apart and disappear altogether and you will once again be alone, having now forgotten how you ever had the strength to travel alone in the first place.

If I am not careful my entire life is going to have passed me by without me having given enough thought to where I am heading. For me there will be no starting again; my final destination will be precisely that, so it

would make sense to go to my rock more often, and make time to think. It's not that I am terribly unhappy – in fact my life is extremely comfortable – it's just that it is when things seem most comfortable that I am most apprehensive, because in comfort, mistakes are made. I liken life to being on a moving walkway at an airport, as soon as you place your first step on its surface you have yielded all control over your destination – it is marked out ahead of you.

Please hold on to the handrail.

What if you suddenly decide you want to get off? What if you see your gate going past and realise you have made a mistake? Too late. You think:

I reckon if I turned around and ran I could move backwards and make it back to where I started ... and there are so many people behind me. They will stare and tut and laugh. At best I will succeed only in maintaining my current position, just beyond where I want to be, but close enough to see what I am missing out on.

Balding men in their sixties who drive convertible sports cars with the roof down in bad weather, women in their fifties who wear too much make-up and too little of everything else in clubs and bars on Wednesday nights, people in their twenties who put off getting jobs and stay at their parents' home all day watching children's television and eating crisps; they are all running

backwards along the walkway and we are all laughing at them.

In my head I unwrap my sandwiches, tear off a piece of crust and drop it into the river, watching it as a parent watches a child taking its first faltering steps. As if immediately overwhelmed by its newfound independence it travels at first only along the water's edge and is pulled into a rock pool by the side, where it swirls round and round, seemingly trying desperately to cling to the back wall. I can almost hear its screams. After a while it is thrown back out and is carried away down river, oblivious of what lies ahead and powerless to struggle against the current. Ham and mustard, if anyone is interested.

But I am not there now – I am in a service-station car park taking deep breaths and trying to calm myself down for having missed something far less beautiful than a sunset but somehow no less important. What an idiot I am.

Gemma represents something more meaningful which I hope will allow me to forget about this sort of thing entirely. If there were someone here I cared about then perhaps none of the other stuff would matter – the order of my coat hangers, the last mouthful of my breakfast, the display on my dashboard. I need some perspective. Nobody has died – there is no prize for seeing your dashboard display at 50,000 miles.

For now though, even thinking about it while trying to calm myself down annoys me. I might never get to see that again.

The way some people feel about birdwatching, I feel about round numbers. Missing the 50k makes me feel as though I were on a birdwatching weekend and as I bent down to tie up my shoelaces a golden eagle flew over me with a dodo in its claws screeching the Macarena. There is only achievement – tasks completed properly or otherwise. I have failed to execute this journey properly and there is a price to be paid.

Closing the door of my car and locking it behind me (this time in silence, I am too angry for silly sentences now), I head indoors to the cafeteria. The chattering ladies behind the service-station counter bring me back once again to the time when I worked as a hotel breakfast cook as a student and I had my first lesson in how incapable I would be in life at maintaining what other people seem able to do easily for hours, namely talking crap. As if a bolt of conversation provides a shock as strong as that from a defibrillator and following the zombified journey into work, on arrival the people in the suits and uniforms perk up at the prospect of a chat about last night's telly. I would arrive at work and maintain roughly the same stony-faced outlook throughout the morning, while all around me cackles and howls from the mouths of waiting and

reception staff bounced off the walls and battered me senseless.

'Did you watch Nigella last night? I'm going to do that Moroccan salad this weekend. I don't know how she isn't five hundred stone with all that food she sneaks down to munch on in the middle of the night!'

'I know! And did you seeeeeeee the size of her pantry!'

Then, the next five minutes were spent giggling at the fact that someone misheard and thought they were talking about the size of her panties. By the time they had all got their breath back it would be time for a cup of tea and a collective harmonious sighing session, like a flock of brooding pigeons, which is a clandestine way of saying, 'Can you believe we get paid for this? What are we like? Oh, it's too much!'

I quite agree. It is as if Britain is filled with conversational diabetics, and knowing that they will be deprived of their supply for eight hours overnight they have a huge booster shot of inane chat before they leave and a life-saving top-up burst on the following mornings. I can only assume that once they left the hotel they didn't speak to anyone all night, sitting in silence like monks in front of *Strictly Come Celebrity Dog Training on Ice.* I'm sure they all thought I was rude, a pompous student too good to talk to ordinary folk, but it wasn't like that.

It had nothing to do with class or intellect – I just didn't know what to say. I once had an opinion on a

programme I had seen, in which Nigella talked us through how to prepare a 'chip butty', but someone spoke in the gap I was waiting for and so I was left waiting at the junction with my indicators on. I wished I could have been a part of it and I wish to this day that I had the capability to pass the time of day with someone at a bus stop, talking about everything and nothing at the same time, but the truth is that I could no sooner execute a session of pleasant small talk than I could sit down and play a game of chess with a grandmaster. It is a skill I have never been taught. The banter flies equally rapidly behind the counter here, much faster than the movement of meals over it, at any rate.

It has not escaped my notice that I have ended up in a profession that means I never have to deal with small talk or conversation of any type. Although at gigs I technically work with hundreds of people at a time, everyone but myself is required by etiquette to remain mute throughout the performance. Any interjection is filed as 'a heckle', an aggressive gesture which demands that I make an insinuation about the originator's mother to maintain my control of the room. It is not a sign of decent social awareness to be capable of speaking without interruption or validation for an hour at a time and so in a sense I can convince myself that all stand-up comedians are equally as screwed up as I am.

I order a latte and grab a packet of biscuits from by the till and this time find a perfectly uncluttered table affording me an unobstructed view of the other customers – behind me I can see out onto the motorway itself. Once seated, I scan the room and engage in my hobby of making value judgements about other customers. There are plenty of travelling families in here who look as though they hate one another. I wonder if the parents' happiness was ever so complete that they felt they had to have a new life to share it with, or did they simply have kids to take the focus away from what went wrong?

We all love to stare at people. There is no malice in it, but so much that can be learned by looking at someone for slightly too long, by breaking the 'occasional glancing rule' with which we all secretly comply. We are taught that it is rude to stare, so we have come to look at people very superficially. Nevertheless it can be exciting to get to stare at someone without their knowledge, to look at the expressions they pull when they talk and all the things that tell us the truth about people.

I am momentarily distracted as I hear a female voice nearby, a voice belonging to a woman in her forties or fifties, saying aloud, 'That's crazy, man!' It doesn't befit a woman of her age and I cannot help but make all sort of assumptions about this woman as a result of her use

of language. Most of these assumptions are probably entirely unfair – maybe she intended the expression ironically having heard her children using it – but I cannot help myself.

Then I see a woman who leaves me utterly transfixed, sitting a few tables away and staring out of the window. Leaning back against her chair, her legs slightly bowed, sits a middle-aged woman, attractive for her age, perhaps because of her age, her eyes full of history and emotion. They stare off into the distance as if she is trying to will her body to lift itself and fly at great speed towards the horizon, towards the unknown. She does not look at me, she does not look at anyone; she does not even look down at the coffee she occasionally fumbles for and sips gently. Her features are as if set in stone, eyebrows and lips are pinned still by the fantasy in her mind. Her nostrils flare gently with each breath; she blinks in spite of herself.

I can see that this is a perfect moment in an otherwise tumultuous day/week/year, the sun breaking through the cloud, and feel glad that I am living it vicariously through her. In her head I imagine the air here smells like a newly extinguished candle, a warm fire is crackling nearby and the drink she savours is the finest mulled wine.

I want her to stay that way for ever, but she snaps out of her mood violently as the phone on the table kicks

into life. Lights flash, a tinny jingle plays and its vibrations propel it across the table with a noise like an angry bee breaking wind.

'I'm in the restaurant. Yes. Up the stairs ... Oh, sorry. No, I thought we said we'd meet here ... OK. Sorry. OK, I'll wait here. Shall I get you a ...?'

She puts the phone down on the table and now sits bolt upright glancing routinely over her shoulders at the door until the man she has been waiting for arrives. A tall, well-built man with crew-cut hair, which is greying around the temples, comes in wearing a denim jacket over a white T-shirt tucked over his belly and into a pair of faded jeans. His face is etched with rage and the veins on his temples look fit to burst. Without thinking she stands as he comes in.

'I been outside the bogs for fifteen fucking minutes, you dozy cunt.'

'I'm sorry, I thought we'd agreed to meet here.'

'Well, we fucking didn't, or else I would've fucking been here wouldn't I? Drinking coffee and enjoying myself instead of standing by the shitters like a fucking perverted prick.'

'I'm sorry, do you want a drink?'

'No. You've pissed me off now. You always fucking do this.'

'I'm sorry,' she says for the third time. I can understand now the fear in her eyes, why she longed for the

164

horizon, why she so treasured that silent moment in heaven. How quickly the best things die.

'I don't fucking *neeeeed* your apology,' he growls. 'Drink up so we can get back on the fucking road.'

'Please. Calm down,' she implores.

He stares at her for an uncomfortable amount of time. After a moment she concedes and stares down into her drink, defeated once more and left wondering what kind of evening awaits her.

I think of shouting over, 'Do you know what I don't need? I don't need you bringing your prehistoric coping strategies into my life. Your pathetic aggression at the fact that the world has moved on without you and being a tattooed prick with dirt under his fingernails is no longer enough to get what you want.'

But I say nothing, because I am terrified of confrontation. This woman clearly needs help, I think, or does she? Should I try to protect her? In all likelihood she wouldn't thank me for it. She made her choice. Twenty years ago there was probably a man who loved her, a quiet, unassuming, average-looking man who loved her so much that she lost respect for him. He was overlooked in favour of this piece of shit with a pulse, whose arrogant self-confidence seemed so secure, so exciting to be around. Fuck her, actually. Fuck everyone who thinks they are stuck with the wrong choices they made

– myself included. When the foundations of your house are rotten, you do not paint your living room.

It dawns on me that all people come to take comfort for granted and problems represent the potential for improvement. Once you have achieved your goal of a garden with the greenest grass, all that remains is a shit view. Women do not inherently love bastards, as the saying goes, but know that bastards leave themselves the most room to manoeuvre. If you regularly berate your wife, steal money from her purse and prevent her from seeing her friends then she is bound to be delighted the one day you make her toast in the morning.

'Steve's really trying', she will tell her mum on the phone that night. 'I think we're going to be OK!'

It won't be OK. At best you will break up the next time he shouts at you in the pub, or worse, and you will look back later on the years you wasted from which you cannot extract a single happy memory. Your chance of a better future is happening now, and it passes every moment you decide not to walk away; the worst that could happen is you stay with him for ever. You stay with him because you grow to pity him and see his aggression as a manifestation of his own unhappy upbringing.

It ain't his fault ma, it ain't.

Of course it is. Let him rot. But I'm not being fair, I'm just lashing out mentally at people who have done

nothing wrong and are trying to deal with life the same way I am. I just hate the greyness of all this emotion; why can't there just be a simple answer, like there is to most questions? Anger is clean, anger apportions blame and refuses to accept responsibility so it is a most appealing first response, but I don't want to be angry – I want to be excited, I want to be oblivious to the people around me. Why did I even text Gemma if this future is what is waiting for us? Could I really ever become that man or is it stupid to even consider the possibility? Texting her was a selfish gesture borne out of my own frustrations at eating breakfast alone. She could at least have replied though.

11.42

BACK HOME

Finishing the journey home in almost a daze, I pull into the maze of suburban cul-de-sacs which is the estate I live on. I did call in at the restaurant on the way home and parked up for a few minutes (probably nearer fifteen) to see if she was there. She wasn't. I recognised one of the other waitresses and wondered whether or not she recognised me. If she had, then I suppose my being there might have looked a little less than sane, so I left again and finished the journey. I will have the rest of the day at home to have a quick tidy around and dry out a little. The rain has worsened and is now falling in heavy, fat droplets. As they hit my shirt they leave dark, thin slashes on the fabric like tiny knife holes.

Would I be happy for Gemma to come here without my having tidied up especially first? Is it a display of effort or an attempt to create a false impression of myself. In any case, maybe instead of tidying up for Gemma's potential visit I should mess things up a bit?

Here you go darling, look at the dust on that! I thought you might like it ... I haven't flushed the toilet either in case that would make you feel uncomfortable.

The modern reality is that if Gemma does come back here, it won't be to run a finger across the top shelf of my bookcase to check for dust, but to be wowed by a night of passionate lovemaking. Suffice to say I find it easier to please in the former regard than the latter. I suppose it is this fact that has always meant I was more popular with the parents of my girlfriends than with the girls themselves.

Mothers were wowed by my cleanliness and consideration, by how polite I was and by the fact that I could cook. Fathers were glad that I was polite and followed football, but glad that I was no threat to their male dominance at home. I am not yet old enough for women to be impressed by their parents' opinions of me and so washing-up after Sunday lunches and managing not to swear through a game of scrabble was time wasted.

'You've got yourself a real keeper there, love,' mothers would coo as I left.

'I've got a slipper-wearing loser whose soul is at least twice the age of his meagre body,' would be the unspoken response.

I should have been stealing her away on a motorbike and telling her parents to piss off, I suppose, because

that's what being young is for. Women have a lifetime ahead of them to settle for someone safe and reliable.

I turn the key in the lock and smile as it clicks open. I had locked the door after all, of course I had. I kick the door open with my toe and a warm gust of air rushes out to greet me with its arms outstretched. The specific combination of aromas assures me immediately that this is my home and there is no other like it. I allow myself to bathe in its familiarity briefly before stepping inside, out of the rain into the porch area. Welcome home.

As I pull the UPVC door closed behind me the sound of the latch clicking into place sends a shiver of elation down my spine. Now I am safe. Now things are back on my terms. No one can look disapprovingly down on me in here, and there is no background music or shouting. I can ignore knocks at the door, unplug the telephone, draw the curtains and disappear for ever if I want to, or at least for the next few glorious hours. Beyond that and my silence would cause problems. People wouldn't notice for a while after, but the peaceful tranquillity would be broken by my paranoid mind. I probably won't want to disappear for ever, in fact, but that option should be available to all of us. That's what home is: home is where no one can get you.

Stooping down to collect the small pile of leaflets and free newspapers that have been delivered in my absence

I get angry about the waste of paper. It seems a double whammy that not only are trees being cut down to make leaflets, but that those leaflets are aimed at convincing me to buy food that is of no nutritional value whatsoever. Cutting down nature to promote crap.

You might as well eat yourself into an early onset coronary, as there won't be enough oxygen left for everyone soon. Chow down. Call now and we'll deliver a pizza the size of a truck's wheel with chips and coke for only £9.99.

Before cutting down a tree a proposal should be submitted in writing to the government to describe what is intended to be printed on something that used to not only live a life of its own, but facilitate ours.

Takeaway leaflets – no.

Shitty comedians' self-involved ramblings? Hmm. A sticking point.

Then, I notice a brown package lurking underneath the crap. Rectangular, lightweight, about the size of a DVD and most probably a DVD. Whilst I have no recollection of ordering anything, sadly that has no bearing whatsoever on whether or not I did. It is far more likely that in a drunken stupor I have gone online and ordered something I thought I needed, only to wake up with no recollection of having done so. Nowadays I don't even need to be sober enough to enter my payment details, the process is so fast.

BACK HOME

Hello Jon! Back again at 3am. What is it this time? Something a little obscure in a foreign language that you'll never watch, or are we drunk enough that you are ordering a film you have loved since childhood without any awareness whatsoever of the fact that you already own three copies?

To be honest this is not the worst habit I have, and it's not even a practice I am altogether unhappy with, since it results in this moment: receiving an unexpected pick-me-up gift from myself! Here you go, mate, I thought I might like this … Ooh! What could it be? Thank me ever so much. I'll open it when I get settled in the lounge.

For now it is enough simply to lean against the back of the door and breathe slowly and deeply, not caring as the rain drips from my hair and runs down my back. The sound of the road outside is now muffled and distant, unable to make itself heard above the ticking of the clock in the hallway, clean and constant. I am becoming more and more myself with each clearly marked-out second that passes. You have to look after number one, that's what everyone else does. Shut the door and make them all go away; do what you need to do to get through the rest of the day. That is the feeling I get when I close my front door – the tragedies continue outside, but in here all is well.

The comfort really comes from the knowledge that this is no temporary state of refuge. I am not seizing upon these moments of stillness because at any moment I expect my housemate might return from work, or my wife and children from school. This feeling of security is the result of much painstaking effort on my part, slowly severing ties and carefully avoiding any encounter that might lead to the formation of an emotional bond with another person.

Not only is the phone not ringing, it will not ring. Only I know the number to my landline and, since I know exactly where I am, I have no need to check up on myself. I drop my keys in their bowl, switch off my mobile phone and throw that in next to them, before hanging my coat on the one strong metal hook in the wall. I usually go for long periods without speaking to people and they wait a few days and then pretend that they have been worried about me when really they have been with girlfriends and wives. I will tell them I'm fine and they'll leave it at that, or sometimes they'll probe and keep asking me what is the matter.

Buzz buzz buzz.

God, it seems like weeks ago that I woke up listening to the shouting coming from next door. I wonder if they have made up yet. Maybe this time they'll really break up and go their separate ways, then either realise how much they loved each other or lament not having done

174

it sooner. Or, in the worst-case scenario, one wants a reunion and the other wants to move on, probably already has actually.

I've been seeing him for a few weeks. Sorry, I didn't know how to tell you, but it hasn't been good for so long between us. It's not you, it is me. You'll be better off without me.

Now that I am at home I feel a possessive sense of pride in my things. It's not that I have any great emotional attachment to them, but I can't wait to see them all again. I long to touch my remote controls, eat with my cutlery, sit in my chair as if I have been away for years; like when you find old T-shirts in summer and forget that you had ever even owned them because the winter was so long. I revel in the absolute certainty that everything in my house is where it was when I left, if perhaps a little dustier.

A niggling doubt tugs at my new-found comfort, tainting it, and I remember that there is some washing up waiting for me on my desk. Never mind, that will soon be dealt with, and then the house will be in total equilibrium.

To most people, self-sufficiency is about growing your own vegetables or keeping chickens, but I think you can rely on a grocer for that. To me, true self-sufficiency is a much more spiritual endeavour, an ability to do without being around people altogether. If

someone told you that the door behind you was locked for ever and meals would be sent to you through a chute, books provided on request and there was a big television in the corner, but you could never see another person again, how would you feel?

No hugs after a bad day at work, no idle chit-chat over the breakfast coffee, no reassuring smiles across crowded rooms full of strangers. The test of total independence comes each night when the bedroom door closes behind you, the lights go out and all that there is to keep you company in the infinite darkness are your thoughts. For most people this is a time of dread, when problems from the day that were glossed over at the time come back to the surface.

Should you have been more sympathetic when you heard about Sarah's uncle's cat's illness? Will she think you don't care or will she understand that you have a lot on at work these days?

Was it necessary to smack Toby to make him go upstairs for a bath earlier? Are you a bad parent or is that sometimes the only way to make him understand? Weren't you smacked as a child and did it not do you no harm whatsoever? But surely the fact that you remember it means it has left some more permanent mark than was ever intended?

What excuse will you use to get out of lunch with your parents this weekend? It's not that you don't love them

– of course you love them – but there is so much to do at home and why should it always be you who has to go around just because you live closest? Would it kill Steve and his family to come up even once a month? They're his fucking parents too, right?

She is going to leave me.

People are not the solutions to all this misery, but the causes of it. Those who care the most experience the most pain. If you are so foolish as to feel empathy and to want the best for the people around you, then they will upset you during the day and keep you awake at night, unless of course you have had enough to drink. To be selfish and deluded is truly a rare gift. I imagine that those whose concerns are only for themselves sleep well enough.

My own may seem a selfish gesture, locking myself away from people who may need *my* help, who might crave *my* company in order to further their own search for happiness. Perhaps it is, but I can say with a sound conscience that I have done my best by those I cared for and it still wasn't enough. I am sure that the decision I made was the right one. How many of us can say that?

Whatever other problems I have in my life as a result of the decision I took, this is where I remind myself that it was the right thing to do. I could stand here for hours, listening to the sound of the rain beating against the door but unable to break through, the wind whistling

through the keyhole, a siren's call trying to lure me outside. Nothing can get in here. In here there is just the still, warm air, those familiar smells and the perfect tick-tock of the hallway clock. And a light. A pulsating, red light further down the corridor.

You have no new messages.

I leave my coat behind on the hook and take my bag into the office and place it by the desk. My laptop sits perfectly in the centre of the table, alongside my note-pad, my diary and a pen, all parallel to one another and equidistant from the edge of the table. The laptop lies open on the table and as I touch a key the light from the screen illuminates an empty chair. The internet window is open and a half-composed email is shown on the screen.

'Hiya mate. Could you get someone to—'

Could who get someone to what? Why didn't I finish the message I wonder? There isn't even a name in the address bar. Had I been drunk or distracted? I close the window and shut down the computer. It can't have been urgent or I would have remembered – I always remember the important things. But what if it was?

Could you get someone to look at this rash on my arm?

Could you get someone to get me the number of the girl who looked after me at that gig last week?

Could you get someone to help me, please?

178

Priority number one is the washing up, so with the dirty mug taken from my desk I head to the kitchen and start running some hot water. The washing up is a singular task, existing independently of my attempts to write a book or any other task to which I have committed myself: my tax return, the payment of my mortgage, my upcoming tour. It is a task that needs to be completed and, having been started, needs to be finished perfectly.

A perfect finish to the washing up means every item in the kitchen is clean (including the hob), the surfaces have been scrubbed with an antibacterial wipe and the sink is free from debris, be that grains of rice, unidentifiable silt or the soapy suds which sit on top of the water surface and stubbornly refuse to drain away. Apart from leaving the task incomplete, they will leave a mark around the edge of the sink if I let them win. The kitchen must be completely clear.

Dirty, dirty, dirty. I haven't shaved for over a week, but things like that don't count. I can't explain to you why they don't count, they just don't. Besides, there is a lot of tidying to do; I have become rather remiss! I am a twentieth-century man, by which I mean that I can change batteries but not tyres, and I take extended warranties and buy replacements rather than take things back to the shop for fear of the embarrassment of being told that all I need to do to mend the item is change the plug.

Oh, of course, yeah, change the plug. I usually do it every day – must've forgotten to do it this morning amidst all the shagging and watching rugby league. What do I change it into exactly?

Maybe none of us are proper men. Maybe we all get caught off-guard every now and again by a surprisingly practical or intelligent point and have to repress the urge to high five every other man in a five-mile radius.

I did it! I just correctly identified the sound of a slipping fan belt on a passing Mini Metro! Holy shit, touch me!

There are just a few other items from last week waiting in the bowl to wash up, mostly teaspoons and one of my cut-crystal whisky glasses. Washing up is the kind of never-ending tedious task that can be a tipping point on days where everything is going wrong. The knowledge that no matter how old I get, I will never be rid of the need to stick my hand now and again into a bowl of tepid water and swirl my hands around the inside of a pan caked with cold bean juice is always a morbid realisation.

You can't cheat things like that – you don't graduate from them. As much as I hated school I knew that one day it would be over and I would never have to go back, and still to this day I wake up from a nightmare in which I haven't done my homework and grin inanely

for hours at the thought that never again will Mr Porter have the chance to chastise me for losing my calculator. I never even did lose my calculator, ever.

Plunging a mug into the water a little too forcefully, a wave of washing-up water swells up inside the bowl and leaps over the side. I leap backwards to avoid it but that only means it slops down onto the floor. Reaching for a few sheets of kitchen towel I bend down to mop it up and look to my left and through the door of the washing machine. I had always assumed the glass on the door was frosted, but this close up I realise that it looks more like a coating of powdery residue.

I open the door and wipe at it with the now soggy kitchen towel and it comes away eventually to reveal clear, shining glass. How had I always missed that? And *who* was I going to email to ask for something? I get an antibacterial wipe from the drawer in which I keep cling film and tin foil and things like that and set to scrubbing the back of the washing-machine door. It feels amazing – the dirt comes away easily and leaves behind a beautifully smooth surface, quite literally as good as new. I toss the dirty wipe into the bin.

Tomorrow is bin-collection day.

I should put rubbish straight into the wheelie bin outside rather than allow it to build up inside. I retrieve the wipe and head off to the front door. I am just unlocking the front door when I notice that there is a spider in

181

the corner of the ceiling; I don't want it to run away while I am outside, or more to the point I don't want it to drop on my head while I am opening the door, so I put the wipe next to the bowl with my keys in it and go upstairs to get something to get rid of my unwanted, eight-legged guest with. I keep an old measuring jug for this purpose in a cupboard under the sink.

On my way through the living room into the kitchen I notice that the Henry is out in the corner of the room, so I must have started hoovering in here at some point yesterday too. Why didn't I finish any of the jobs I started? I don't know why I'm talking in the past tense, I'm doing exactly the same thing now. The washing up isn't even half-finished and I'm already in the middle of three other things.

Then the point at which I stopped working last night comes back to me in a flash and I remember kicking the Henry into the corner of the room, calling it a 'fucking prick' and pouring a large brandy. It's not my fault I talk to Henry – the manufacturers gave it a face and a name, not me. *Thou shalt call each thing by its right name.*

While I was hoovering in the living room I had needed to move the side table by the settee, which I noticed still had last week's old TV guide on it. I had picked it up and replaced it with the new one that was on the seat next to where I sit, but when I went to put the old guide with the other old papers in the bag that

hangs in my airing cupboard I found that the bag was full so I needed to take it outside and put it in the green bin. Then when I came back something must have got in the way again.

How can trying to make things tidier mean so much more mess?

I like alcohol because, unlike other drugs, it does not alter my reality. Alcohol doesn't make things look different or make me giggle like a moron for no reason; it just stops some of the extra thoughts I don't seem able to push out when I'm sober.

The spider is still there.

I drink almost anything at home – I even have a revolving optic like they use in bars to pour even measures of spirits. I keep whisky, brandy, gin and vodka on mine and when I can't decide which I want to drink I play a game called 'Spin and Win!' in which I spin the optic and drink a shot of whichever spirit points at me when the motion has stopped. It's called Spin and Win basically because I spin it and no matter which way it points I win!

When I go in to the kitchen and pick up the glass a sudden urge hits me to lob it with full force against the wall, shattering it into as many pieces as possible and shattering along with it all my pent-up rage. Before I can even pull my arm back behind my head he chips in.

Don't do that.

And I put the glass down on the side again.

If you smash that glass, you will just have to go and clear it up again. It serves no purpose.

I know this thought is supposed to be a positive one but that won't help with the anger inside me. Before I have even had the chance to be reckless, it has been taken away from me by my crushing rationality. Now smashing the glass has ceased to be a moment of abandonment as it would be for anyone normal and has become a considered decision. If I am aware of the consequences then I must take full responsibility for them.

However it might make me feel, smashing a glass against the wall will only pose a health and safety risk, create more work for myself and rob me of one of my nice glasses. I might just as well cut out the work aspect and neatly place one of my glasses into the bin, but even to me it is clear that this represents total madness. Of course I would have to wrap it up in newspaper first so that the bin-collection men weren't injured when taking my rubbish away.

The rubbish is still in the hallway.

Perhaps I could drive out to the middle of nowhere with the glass as my hostage and smash it against a tree, before driving home again?

What if a badger or a fox ran over the glass and cut their feet? How would you feel then?

I know very well that this is the part of my brain that stops me shouting at strangers on trains or sticking my hand into the fire just to see what it feels like, but right now it isn't helping. The daemon of my rage is still by my side, prodding at me and daring me to do something stupid to get it out of my system. Next time I will just throw the glass before the other voice can interrupt. I feel a sudden shiver down my back and my hands are getting twitchy so I put the glass calmly back on the side, pour a brandy into another less expensive glass and go and sit in the bath for a bit.

There is a common misconception that there has to be hot water and bubbles in the bath for sitting in it to be an enjoyable experience, but I find that if I put on my big dressing gown, and climb in with the door closed and the lights off and put a big towel over my body, I can feel quite safe and hidden in it anyway for a little while, in which time I can get my head together again.

The walls of the bath box me in and I can just get to grips with the small area I am in before I start to think about anything else. It smells nice in here, like soap, and by curling up and tucking my knees into my chest and clutching them into position with my arms, with my eyes closed I feel like nothing can get me. There are no problems in the bathroom so everything immediately around me is fine.

I think back to a technique I developed at university for helping me cope when there seemed too much to sort out; a technique I called 'zooming'.

University is where people go to 'find themselves' which is all well and good, but it should not be assumed that you will like what you discover there. I moved away from home only to find that I was a fastidious misanthrope who was more concerned with the cleanliness of a cutlery drawer than finishing an essay on the rise of Fascism and its role in the Spanish Civil War.

Whilst at university I would sneak out onto the balcony of our apartment block with a can of cheap lager when the stress got too much, and out there I developed a coping strategy I called 'The Zoom Technique'. I would begin by focussing as intently as I could on everything that was bothering me, in as much detail as possible and listing everything I could think of, before speculating on what things might be bothering the four people I shared an apartment with at the time.

Pressures of work, family, relationships that I knew of and others that I didn't. After that I would imagine how many problems must have been on the minds of all the people in our building, before once again zooming out to include everyone on the campus. It seemed impossible that someone on the campus didn't have far bigger problems to deal with than I did.

After that I would consider everyone at Bristol University, then everyone in Bristol, everyone in England, and then Europe and finally the whole world. By this point I swear I could feel the collective weight of violent relationships, famine, war and illnesses forcing me down into the ground. I would then remind myself that none of the problems outside of my own was my responsibility; they were not my fault. All I had to deal with were the things that were bothering me in the first place, perhaps a bit of mess, some deadlines and the fact that I missed my family. It all seemed so easy to fix then.

I would carry out this exercise whenever I felt the need and it never once failed to help me feel better. I suppose this is the same theory that nowadays stops me from switching on the news in the morning because I have forgotten that I am not responsible for the problems of the world ... but am I doing anything to help alleviate them?

I am not unaware of the unimportance of what I do for a living. Comedy is not an essential job – it does not save lives or protect people. I do what I do because I am allowed to and I am well rewarded for it, but I feel guilty that I am not doing anything more worthy and so I cannot bear to hear about the problems that used to alleviate my stress.

Back then I was just a student, still finding my way and still unable to express any influence over my own decisions, let alone suspect I may have influence wider afield. Now I am older (though not nearly old enough to feel as weary as I do!) but I have moved into the category of 'dream achiever'. I have the job I dreamed of as a child and I thought it would bring me eternal happiness, but if anything it has made me feel worse.

Dreams are an excuse for unhappiness; they allow us to think we would be happier and healthier if only we had what we were looking for. Once that thing has been found and eternal bliss remains as unattainable as ever, then unhappiness takes on a life all of its own, unconnected to any one possession or person. It is an entity that cannot be controlled, cannot be defeated and comes and goes from your life entirely as it pleases like a drunken guest at a house party, staggering from room to room and bringing with them only chaos.

Though the Zoom Technique may have helped me get through some tough nights in my teens, looking back now I guess I can identify it as the planting of the seeds which would later become my perfectionism and lust for complete control over my life. University itself represents the first time that you are put in control of your own life and possessions, away from the family home. Until then most of the things at home had been

simply the way they were – that was the remote-control table, that was where tea towels were kept and so on. It wasn't that they were right or wrong, but just how they were.

At university however, in your own flat, everything has to be put away for the first time and therefore thought has to be put into the proper way to do this, as the system to be used, once implemented, would maintain itself. These were not just tea towels – these were *my* tea towels! I remember feeling somewhat guilty about the excitement I felt about this prospect. Of course I was nervous about leaving home and sad to be living so far from my family, but I was also excited by the thought of owning my own chopping boards, of doing my own laundry and of having my own systems.

For my mum, there was no consolation – she was simply watching her son leave home and I will always find it difficult to forgive myself for making that situation worse by making her feel unable to help me set up my new home. As she began unpacking clothes and putting them on hangers ready to go into the wardrobe, I must have unintentionally given her a look of discomfort that stopped her from going any further.

'You probably want to do this yourself, don't you?' she asked through quivering lips, eyes set back behind smeared mascara. 'You'll only end up having to do it all again if I do it.'

'It's just … They need to face forward in the wardrobe with the hooks going over the front,' I said, 'and T-shirts with T-shirts. You know?'

'Sorry.'

And with that she sat on the end of the bed and focussed her energies on trying not to look upset in case it made me feel guilty about leaving home. Families that are sensitive to each other's needs can sometimes be a mess of inactivity as nobody wishes to offend anyone else by making a decision they fear might be motivated by their own desires. There have been times when my sister, mother and I have gone back and forth for hours trying to second guess the secret desires of the others before reaching a conclusion that pleases none of us, simply to avoid only pleasing one of us!

I knew at the time I was making things worse but I couldn't seem to control my urge to have things organised properly getting in the way of not hurting people I cared about. If she had put books on shelves she might not have done it alphabetically, and if she had put the jam away the labels on the jars might not all be facing the front; so because of my stubbornness she felt helpless and did nothing.

I hated upsetting my mother over something I knew to be trivial, but I didn't seem able to help myself. To this day I put my mother under undue pressure to do

things the way I have decided they should be done. She is someone who thinks nothing of digging her knife into her margarine when she is making toast, whereas I slide my knife gently across the top of it, scraping off what I need but leaving the surface smooth and intact.

The rational part of me knows that there is really no difference and certainly no 'right' or 'wrong' way of buttering your own toast, but I have reacted with such pain when taking the lid off her spread that she now smoothes over the top of her margarine when she knows I am coming to visit! It is absolutely insane to think that I could have made her feel so self-conscious about the appearance of the inside of a tub of hydrogenated fat in her fridge and worrying as to how much else she might alter in her own home to prepare for one of my visits.

My mother is a small woman, and as kind and generous a person as you could hope to meet. She deserves to live at peace in her own home and I hate the thought that a visit from her own son could drive her to feel even a moment's discomfort.

I have gone on to annoy and upset friends and girlfriends in much the same manner, but I stand by my systems, even if other people refuse to stand by me as a result. I can't seem to want to change enough to actually do it though and despite all the arguments I still believe in the old adage 'a place for everything and

everything in its place'. When I come home at night exhausted by the world outside, the least I expect is that all my things will be where I left them on my way out. If I wanted my things to move at random without my touching them I would live on a boat.

One thing of which I cannot accuse my mother, and which I will go so far as to say is definitely wrong, is leaving crumbs in her margarine. That was a horror I discovered in my second spell of shared accommodation, living with three other comedians. Opening a jar of marmite and thinking that someone had accidentally dropped half a scotch egg into it is not an experience I wish to repeat, not to mention opening a jar of pickled onions that I had been saving for a special occasion (don't get me started) to discover that it is actually a jar of onion-flavoured vinegar, or clearing away a mug from the living-room floor that had been used as a receptacle for some toe-nail clippings. The logistics of even getting them into the cup baffles me and I almost wish I knew how it had been done, but when I think about it in detail I start dry retching.

All the time I lived with other people the cleaning still seemed to come down to me. I suppose it was largely because I didn't see cleaning as something that either could or couldn't be done – I saw it as something that had to be done. There is, I now understand, an alternative view that cleaning is something that some

people enjoy and others do not, like olives, and that those who do not enjoy it can simply live without it.

In this latter world, cups simply find their way back into the kitchen and teaspoons, like bacteria, are able simply to reproduce at will, dividing and multiplying endlessly to fill the void left by the disappearance of their brothers and sisters. I may sound as though I am being patronising here and I hope that is the case, because I mean to.

If you have reached full adulthood without learning that if you enjoy and use milk, then at some point milk must be purchased and kept in cold storage somewhere within reach of the user, then you deserve to be spoken down to. Of course people are aware of these facts but it is easier to pretend not to be than to admit, 'Well, of course I know I haven't bought milk since 1988, but the shop is always outside and my desire for a cup of tea is always inside, so I find it easier just to use yours!'

There really are only two solutions to this problem:

1. Accept that you will always be the one who buys the milk. A sad admission of defeat but ultimately, almost like Buddhist teachings, it is better simply to accept the way of things and focus your energies on other tasks than to try to change the direction of the wind by blowing against it with all your might.

2. Refuse to buy milk or tidy up until someone else
   does it, with the result that you will end up living
   in a milkless hovel and die of scurvy or
   something similar.

On the few occasions that I tried to hold out longer than
my old flatmates, a period I came to call 'my fairy liquid
embargo' during which I kept the basic essentials for
existence hidden away in my bedroom and left communal areas to descend into whatever state was deemed
appropriate by the mob, it was still me who caved in
first as they found ever more ingenious ways to get
round the problems, from the very simple decision to
effectively move back in with their parents, eating all
meals there and sleeping there, to making a game of
finding more and more ingenious ways of getting food
from the packet and into their mouths.

Of course only a mind as rigid and inflexible as mine
would assume that cereal had to be eaten from a bowl,
and that when there were no clean bowls one would be
washed up. Oh, how naive! Cereal can be eaten just as
effectively from a measuring jug, soup can be poured
into 24 different shot glasses and knocked back like
tequila and tea can be drained slowly into the mouth
through an old, dirty sock if the situation calls for it.

Takeaway food provided another avenue for escape
and I ended the war when empty pizza boxes covered

the living-room floor entirely. It began to look a little too much like crating for me to feel at all comfortable, and since I was also refusing to buy toilet roll I feared it was only a matter of time before they began to defecate in the corners of the room and bury it there.

A recent discussion with one of my old flatmates began with him asking me if I remembered the incident with 'the note', which I am sorry to say that I didn't.

'Oh, you'd remember this one,' he grinned. 'It was a real work of art!'

I began writing notes at university, and fell into the trap of trying to sound like I really wasn't as concerned as it might seem by beginning each one with the words 'Hey guys!'

Hey guys! It'd be really cool if we could all do our washing up when we have finished our dinner, as it's not really fair on those who get in late if there's nothing clean to use. Hope everyone's well. Jon

Which in reality roughly translates into:

Oi, pricks! If I get back from the gym and find that all the fucking pans are dirty once more, I'm going to start pissing on all of you while you sleep. I hope you are as miserable as I am here. Jon

Maybe the second note would have had more of an effect than the faux-friendly, hair-ruffling tones of the first, but I suppose I was trying to retain the moral high ground. The fact that I had to write one of these notes

every week should have been enough of a sign that nobody was paying any attention to them. I am not proud to admit that I have written a number of terse notes in my time, so much so in fact that no one incident seems memorable.

The note that my former flatmate was referring to had been written after a particularly gruelling evening's cleaning while the flat had been unoccupied by anyone but me, perhaps at the end of a long-term cleaning embargo. Before going to bed I apparently wrote a detailed note outlining all the cleaning that I had done that evening, how long each task had taken and a sum total of my time spent. After researching the current minimum wage I calculated a fee for my work, divided it by three and issued each of them with a bill for my services.

I wish I could have shown you a copy of this note, but even I will admit that had I written this note and then also kept a copy on file in my private records for future reference, I shouldn't be here writing down the details of the incident for you but should be in a secure unit somewhere taking the green pills at breakfast and the red ones at lunch.

Always the green pills at breakfast, isn't that right, Mr Richardson? He used to be a comedian you know? Yes, in London! He's on that there youtubes, not that you kids will remember that.

The most upsetting part of this story is that I can't for the life of me remember doing it. I can only assume that I entered some sort of maniacal state beyond consciousness. I picture myself in an apron on my hands and knees scrubbing a bathroom floor cackling to myself in a way not unlike Muttley from the Wacky Races and conducting full conversations with the cartoon on the front of the Mr Muscle bottle.

After a year spent living that way I could only conclude that it was me that had the problem. Eventually the maths seems simple: three messy-living men with girlfriends (how they had girlfriends I couldn't understand) against one note-writing lunatic loner put me in the minority, so it must be me who needed to assimilate with them rather than the other way around. I hated the fact that my friends were seeing me as someone even I couldn't stand to be with – a moaning, pernickety twat who bears grudges and harbours resentment – so I left.

It was at that point that Swindon seemed like my best option, away from everything. You only get one chance for people to see you as perfect and the longer and longer you can maintain that image the greater the pressure on it. I could never go back to being a person they could respect so I had to get further away and try to rebuild slowly. It was my inflexible perfectionism and black and white understanding of things that

isolated me from my friends, and continues to this day to do so.

When, only a year into my studies and inexplicably miserable, I dropped out of university in what I was sure at the time was the worst decision I had ever made and would surely commit me to the scrapheap for the rest of my life, I had to pack up all the things I seemed to have only recently put in place. Every item that I boxed up was another brick in the wall of my failure and placing each item allowed me another moment's reflection.

A book in the box. *Are you sure this is right?*

Another book in the box. *Are you actually going to put this away and leave here altogether?*

A third. *Really, Jon? It isn't too late to take it all back.*

The task seemed to go on for ever and I longed for it to be over so I could start again somewhere else. When it came to emptying my wardrobe I put my open palms at either end of the wardrobe, facing one another, and brought them firmly together lifting out every item in one satisfying movement. Clutch, up and out. A clean break. Perfectly clean. Worth upsetting your mum over? I'm not sure.

If my personality has cost me my place at university, my relationship and the chance to live with my friends, it was this third failure that hurt the most. I had proved incapable of finishing university, but there were thousands like me every year, I was sure. I had failed in love, or at least with my first 'proper' girlfriend, but that was somehow beyond my control – something higher and beyond reach was in charge of that. But the fact I had been unable to live even with my best friends really hurt.

Friendship was something that transcended physicality; it was almost purer than any love you could feel for a partner. The friends you make as a child who stay with you throughout your life do so not because they find you attractive, or they gain financially from your time together, but because something deep down connects the two of you. Because you have stayed with each other through more than one period of your evolution. The fact that my thoughts and ways had sullied even that meant that I would have to learn to depend only on myself for contentment, that I would have to learn to cope with being totally on my own.

I moved away to a place where I knew nobody and where I thought nobody would come. I switched my phone off and didn't respond to messages. People would ask what was wrong and I would tell them I had a problem with my phone; I just wouldn't tell them that the problem was that having it turned on made me feel frightened and sick. I had to learn to find happiness for myself, but is that even possible?

★ ★ ★

Perhaps I can still use the old 'zoom' method to make myself feel better. I start in the bathroom and then cover the hallway, then the kitchen and lounge and then I can't cope because there is already too much mess.

It isn't long before I notice I can hear the clock ticking in the hallway and I know that nothing can stop time from moving on. I have to 'man up' as the Americans call it. No one is going to do it for me so if I just run around frantically for five minutes and try not to get distracted I can put everything back into place.

Folding the towel neatly and placing it back on the hanger, on my way out of the bathroom I grab a handful of clothes from the laundry basket. There might be some white stuff in there but in all honesty it doesn't matter what the colours are since I haven't bought any new clothes in so long that there is no chance of any colours running anyway.

I head into the kitchen and put them in the machine with a tablet from under the sink and switch it on for a thirty-degree quick wash. While in the kitchen I wash the few remaining items on the side and place them on the drainer. I sprint into the living room and move the table back where it was and just put the hoover away without finishing the job – that will have to wait until later; the place is relatively dust free anyway.

Then I go downstairs to put the recycling out for the morning with the rubbish bag and the spider is gone. I

stupidly pretend it doesn't bother me but since there is no one around to notice this show of bravado, I might as well just admit that this will also keep me awake tonight.

When I come back in I lock the door and feel satisfied that sooner or later everything looks to be in shape. Everything seems to be finished.

You poured all the water away, but the bubbles are still there.

There is always something else to worry about.

I wonder what it would be like if there were actually nothing left to finish and realise that in a perverse way I am happiest when furthest from completion. When there is so much to be done, so much tidying to do at home and in my mind, I have no option but to knuckle down and get on with it, and the results of my efforts are quickly visible. The closer I get to finishing, the more vague the work becomes and actually it becomes a question of maintaining what you have rather than bettering things. Maintaining perfection is an impossible battle. This is why I haven't let myself enter into a relationship for eight years, so that there is always a glass on the sideboard. Maybe I am afraid that when I get everything I want I will just disap- pear, like a computer game that has been finished, or worse still I will have a life so perfect that the future can only mean heading downhill and losing the things I care for.

On my way out of the kitchen, the bubbles now rinsed away and everything seeming complete, I pull the bookcase that stands against the wall down behind me, so it crashes against the floor, spilling its contents everywhere and gouging deep lines out of the plaster-board walls behind it.

Without stopping or turning around to look at the damage, moving silently as I do so, I kick the nest of tables back towards the kitchen, the lamp goes flying and the TV guide flops down on to the floor. It all feels so good that I start laughing until I collapse backwards on to the floor with a huge sigh of relief.

While I am lying on my back, there is a knock at the door but I ignore it. I know they know I am here, but I also know they won't do anything but leave.

Is it her? Is it Gemma? Nonsense – she doesn't know where I live.

What the fuck did you do all that for?

I am my own boss. Don't worry about the mess – I'll sort that out tomorrow. Put it on the list. I think I need to get out of the house for a while. Why hasn't she texted me back? And why haven't I heard from my agent?

Spoon, jar … jar, spoon. Girl, book … book, girl. Probably best to get out of the house for a while. Some exercise, perhaps?

13.24

GYM'LL FIX IT

A few paces before I reach the door to my local gym, I get my membership card ready in advance to prevent any awkward fumbling in the foyer in front of the attractive girl who usually lurks by the reception. Even such a small task as this is made easier by systems that have been put in place and perfected over many years. My wallet is always kept in my right trouser pocket (keys in the left, phone in the back left-hand pocket except when an inside jacket pocket is available). A black leather wallet, plain and simple but beginning to show signs of wear and tear now, though not quite time for an upgrade.

Once inside the wallet, it opens to reveal those cards which are intended for use on a more-or-less daily basis: debit card and gym-membership card. To the left, behind a little clear plastic window, is my driver's licence. The right-hand section lifts up to reveal less important cards, such as my store reward cards.

I have one such card for each major supermarket chain, which I am quite sure would enrage conspiracy theorists. I hear people complaining that these cards are simply a way for the supermarkets to 'get to know what I buy and when I buy it'. Well, jolly good then! I dream of a day when I can walk into a shop, swipe a card on entry and be told exactly what I need, what else is on offer and what treats I might like based on recent trends. If that increases their profits then so be it, so long as it reduces the time I spend traipsing back up and down the same aisles looking for things and as long as it means I have one fewer list to write in an average week. Kudos to the store loyalty card.

In a concealed section at the back of my wallet I keep one ten-pound note and one ten-euro note, in case of emergencies. I used to keep a condom in here, but I got so tired of transferring the same one across each time I bought a new wallet that the gesture began to depress me too much, in much the same way that it might upset disabled people if wheelchairs had a compartment for storing skis. How could it be long enough to perish leather since I last had call to use this condom? As a man I am required to carry a condom with me at all times, as if the possibility for sex could occur at any moment and with little or no warning. You think you are just nipping to the shop for some bread, but really should accept that you are probably going to end up sleeping with the girl on the checkout and maybe someone else too. Best always to travel tooled up.

I now keep foreign currency in my wallet because sadly it seems to me far more likely that I might suddenly wake up in the centre of Europe without knowing how I got there than that I might end up with a woman in some kind of sexual scenario. I think even describing the occasion as a sexual scenario shows why I don't end up in them more often.

I lack the lingo and the physical presence for generating sexual attraction and nowhere is that more apparent than in my gym. In the three years I have been (irregularly) coming here I have seen men who to begin with were the same size as me but who, through their dedication and love of lifting things above their head, have grown twice as tall and three times as wide as they were.

I, however, seem to be staying roughly the same shape, a kind of pasty white, flat-chested hobbit with sunken shoulders and bad posture. On each flank there is a little promontory of podge above each hip. A wife or significant other would refer to these as love handles, but being as I am single they are simply handles – and handles that somehow make it far less likely that you will be picked up easily.

I like to keep fit simply because I know that when it gets dark and I am climbing into bed my thoughts become negative enough without hating the body that is exposed when I undress. I don't like my face and I

don't like my brain but I don't see that I can do anything about them. However, when I start to put on weight and a paunch develops ahead of me, I see a situation that could be resolved by effort and determination alone and that makes it inexcusable.

It would be easier if supermarkets would cater more for those of us who live alone. It is all too easy now to buy larger and larger packs of food and get them at any time too, since the supermarkets are open twenty-four hours a day – except on Sundays, where God asserts his power by insisting that, despite whatever charity work we might do in our own time, if we buy a courgette after 4pm on the Holy Day we will burn for all eternity in the fires of Hell (though the fact that when I lean forward while driving my belly has started to push me backwards suggests that courgettes are not the most frequent item on my shopping list).

Perhaps my loyalty-card statement would reveal a few too many deep-pan pizzas and not quite enough oranges and lemons. I am not fat by any stretch of the imagination, but punish myself for any physical imperfection because I have no excuse for it. I do not work gruellingly long hours and I am not chained to a desk; my weight fluctuates simply because at times I can be very lazy.

There are days when I can sleep until lunchtime, spend the afternoon on the couch and still sleep

soundly that night. I have to fight to remind myself that advances in medicine mean it is more than possible that my heart will go on beating well into my eighties and possibly beyond, and I do not want my body to have given up the ghost while my mind remains active. This seems a very clinical reason to exercise. I hope the receptionist isn't the attractive girl. I hope it isn't, but I am almost certain that it will be.

It is.

She looks up, half-recognises me and smiles sweetly. She doesn't know who I am, but she knows that she occasionally sees me and this means we are supposed to speak in a tone which suggests personal intimacy, but we are not to exchange any private information.

'Hiya! You alright?'

'Yes, thanks. You?'

'Yeah.'

And so ends the longest period of chat I will have with anyone in Swindon today. This is the conversation I have each time I arrive at my gym, without exception. The same words, mumbled in the same tone, at the same speed and with the same lack of genuine care. The smile disappears as quickly as it arrived and she then looks back down at her computer screen. Classic banter!

I am not sure which I find more depressing, the synthetic three-line chorus of the gym receptionist or the overbearing catalogue of inane questions of what

you would call 'a genuine people person'. I am left annoyed and slightly hurt by the fact that this girl doesn't actually care how I am, nor would she notice if I never came through the sliding glass doors ever again, but would gladly settle for this conversation in place of a barrage of questions from a server whose eyes beg you not to leave their shop. Were there any chance of an interesting conversation with someone who is scanning your items in a supermarket, for example, I would be delighted to chat, but there so rarely is.

'*So* ... (BEEP) *Do you think politicians* (BEEP) *can really make a difference or* (BEEP) *are the new generation of career politicians* (BEEP) *just power-hungry money grabbers? These pizzas are on three-for-two by the way – I'll get Sharon to run over and get you another one, chunky.*'

On the few occasions on which I have found myself trying to instigate some chat, I have seemed to drastically over-estimate the sense of humour of the person I am talking to and ended up offending them in some way. Once while buying my food for the week the cashier told me that the price would be £23.17 before changing her answer to 'Sorry – £32.17'.

'That's pretty hefty inflation,' I wittily retorted. 'Bloody Tories!'

The expression on her face couldn't have shown more surprise if she had looked up to find that I was

driving straight towards her at sixty miles per hour in a two-tonne truck. In general, most of my acerbic political satire at the checkout of my local supermarket falls on deaf ears. Another tip would be that if you ask how long someone has been running their shop, and they reply 'a decade', your next comment should *not* be, 'What did you just call me?'

I do miss having someone to laugh at my jokes, though, and as I have made clear the validation that Gemma's laughter offers me is a large part of why I find her attractive. I think that's why I subject anyone who has the misfortune to serve me in a shop to five minutes of my newest material each time I leave the house. Nothing makes you feel more pathetic than asking the manically depressed emo working on the tills at Boots if he has seen the latest Diet Coke advert, especially if is it 4.30 in the afternoon and those are the first words you have spoken that day.

Walking away from the girl who has already forgotten I exist I pass through another set of doors and enter the locker room. I regularly smash records in the gym, but unfortunately the records broken are less likely to be my time for a ten-kilometre run and more likely to be the record for 'droopiest set of testicles I ever want to see in the flesh'. It seems to be the rule that those with the least to be proud about are often the most willing to put themselves on display. What I am trying to say is that,

while the Crown Jewels may be kept under lock and key away from prying eyes, PoundLand are quite happy to display their stock in a high street window.

Thankfully on a Sunday afternoon, when most people are at home eating roast dinners and watching James Bond movies, the gym is quiet and the changing room is empty as I enter. I can hear a shower running in the back room but there is no one visible. I scan the lockers to locate my favourites.

007 Taken. Always the first to go, ironically.

077 Taken.

100 Taken.

207 Taken. This means that if I were to head back out into the car park, somewhere I would find a Peugeot 207 neatly reversed into its parking space, recently cleaned and with a tree-shaped air freshener hanging from the rear-view mirror. It's not that I know this person specifically, but I can tell by their locker choice that they are like me. There are more of us than it seems – the people who live by rule and order – but we seldom speak of it.

Lockers are very appealing to me, like little safety deposit boxes. I have always been pleased by my ability to shrink things down and feel oddly comfortable in small spaces. As a child I would climb into the airing cupboard and hide among the sheets and towels for hours and as recently as a few years ago, when the stresses of shared accommodation got me down, I would go and spend a night in my car to get away from the mess. My car is my own little mini-hotel.

Synaesthesia is a condition which can mean (amongst other things) that when a 'synaesthete' hears a number, his or her mind conjures a very clear image for each one. Not as simply as a person who hears the number three will imagine a '3', but a far more complex image with a distinct shape, colour and texture. This means that certain numbers can be perceived as more beautiful than others and in such a world phone numbers become much more than a series of digits – they can be vivid clashes of colours and moving shapes.

I feel a jealousy deep within me that I will never have such a personal relationship with the numbers I encounter, but must make do instead with the basic comfort that is brought to me by multiples of five. It is a wonder to me what untapped resources lie within the human brain and furthermore what it is that opens up these avenues of thought that are ignored by most of us. Can willpower alone force the brain into extraordinary action? Do most of us fall short simply because we do not push ourselves far enough, content as we are to take the world at face value?

Without even being aware of it, I seem to have changed into my running gear, folded my clothes neatly into locker 241 and closed the door. This is what ordinary people call 'auto-pilot' but I call 'driving with your eyes closed' because that's more like what it is. It doesn't mean that someone else is in charge and you can take a break; it means you switched off at random in the middle of an important task, with the likely result that an accident is imminent.

One day I will enter autopilot whilst getting changed and snap out of it only in time to realise that I have taken all my clothes off, sealed them into my locker along with the key to the lock and headed up to the gym completely in the buff. I am glad to see that I have chosen a good locker for myself though, opting for 241 because it feels as though I am getting something for free.

It's a locker bogof, so to speak.

I padlock it (whispering to myself, 'Jon is locking his locker and getting two for one as well') and head up to the gym, climbing onto a treadmill over in the corner away from anyone else and away from the mirrors that seem to fixate them so much.

Mirror, mirror on the wall, who is the buffest of them all?

Why it is you, oh fat-necked one … But Snow White split up with you when you were fifteen and her family

eventually moved to Croydon. Do you really think you can get her back now, by lifting heavy things? Tut tut.

It makes sense to me to select a locker whose number I am likely to remember. Who wouldn't forget putting their things in locker 143? What a boring number. My love of individual numbers tends to have more to do with their neatness or the patterns they help create in my mind rather than any kind of synaesthesia.

These are exactly the avenues of thought I am able to explore while I am running and I love poking my nose into every corner of them – *this* is the reason I make myself come here. When I run outside I enjoy the air and the scenery, but I find it hard to switch my brain off as easily as I can on a treadmill.

Outside I can't stop planning routes, looking out for cars, being self-conscious of my breathing and wondering whether I am frightening the old lady I am sprinting towards and hating myself for the possibility. Indoors there are no such problems, there is nothing to think of but putting one foot in front of the other and going on doing so for as long as possible.

My still brain is jagged and messy and demands an answer for each question before it will let me move on to something else, but here things are fluid and soft and while the upper level of my thought is so focussed on breathing and getting oxygen to my muscles, the rest of it can wander wherever it pleases. Thoughts can

mingle and combine to create new colours and new ideas altogether. It is as if rationality is what holds me captive and exercise and alcohol are the only ways to subdue it long enough for me to escape through an open window.

There is also a pleasing neatness to running, a simple question of placing one foot in front of the other to a regular drumbeat and watching the seconds pass by until a specified target has been reached. Targets must be set before stepping foot on the treadmill if they are to stand any hope of being reached. I used to watch television whilst running, on one occasion even spotting a nine-letter word on *Countdown* somewhere in the midst of my fourth kilometre, probably one of the most satisfying and self-righteous thirty seconds of my entire life.

Executing wordplay *and* burning calories? I have the power!

The TV viewing had to end after an incident during a newsflash which showed, from the perspective of the driver, a high-speed crash into the wall during a Formula 1 race. My instinctive reaction was to dive to one side to try to escape the impending impact and what followed was a frantic thirty seconds of scrambling to keep my balance and not crash down on to the fast-moving belt before being spat out into the middle of the room like waste from an effluent pipe. Now I just

look out of the window towards the restaurant over the road.

It pleases me to note that while I am burning calories, people nearby are piling them on. It feels like gaining double the advantage over the other contestants in the human race.

Two for One. TwoFourOne. 241, 241, 241. I am unable to understand how it is that people gain any enjoyment from swimming, or how they could find it in any sense relaxing. There is a distinct difference between exercising and avoiding death by drowning. I have never been good at swimming, because there is no incentive beyond not drowning. If I fall out of a boat, I will survive, but I refuse to start a process of devolution by working my way back into the water.

We began life aquatically and then developed over time the necessary limbs and body parts to live on land. As far as I am concerned if you are a good swimmer then that means simply that you have not yet evolved far enough. I splash and sink and veer off line and cannot help but divert every thought I have towards how uncomfortable I am.

Only on occasion do the things I see penetrate the blissful bubble I enter when I am running. I cannot seem to help but get enraged when I see people parking in the parent and toddler spaces who are clearly neither parents, nor toddlers and certainly not both. I have

thought of complaining to the staff but I don't want the girl at reception to come to know me as a snitch and a jobsworth. *Miss! Miss! They're cheating and it's not fair!*

On the whole, problems begin to unravel themselves subconsciously whilst exercising and I wonder why I make things so difficult the rest of the time. Perhaps this is what it is like to meditate, I wonder, and resolve to take more time to breathe and step back from the problems I generate. I could have put the number card in front of me, with the flower on the opposite side and the salt and pepper to my left and right – it certainly would have done the job until the number card was taken away, but instead I picked at people who were just trying to get through the day, in the same way I am doing when I play traffic wardens on the treadmill.

Some days I feel as though I could run for ever, but there are others that are a constant struggle. Those days are always better once I get through them, but so much harder at the time. Today I am tired almost instantly and my right leg seems more tired than the left. I wonder if this means I am about to have a heart attack and look up at the display to see how close I am to my five-kilometre target.

2.21km

Not even half way. I reach for my drink and take a deep breath but that makes my heart hurt while I

swallow and my brain starts telling me I have to slow down, to walk for a minute and get my breath back. I know better though. This is a trick and if I do that I won't be able to get up to speed again – I have to keep going and get through this brief period of struggle. I make an involuntary noise as I exhale, a short, sharp moan, the kind of noise people in poorly acted films make when they wake up suddenly from a nightmare.

Hurgh!

It helps, though – it makes the struggle real and not just in my head. I begin to imagine that I am a soldier training for a battle in which I must defend my people from the invading forces of evil. People depend on me – women and children – so I have to keep going. Puffing out my chest I open my stride a little and try to settle into a rhythm staring straight ahead.

These battles go on and on until I realise I am approaching the end of my run. For the last few hundred metres I increase my pace to make sure I have the satis-fying feeling of total exhaustion at the end and now everything hurts. The music in my headphones is at top volume and although I can't hear it I am pretty sure I'm making a whole series of unattractive noises now.

Argh! Euch! Heeerrr!

But I don't care – I must defend my people.

When the dial reaches 5km I grab for the speed control and pull right back to walking pace, panting

217

deeply and clutching for the handrails along the sides of the treadmill. Almost instantly I become aware of how red my face must be and what noises I have been making. Now that the fight is over, the negative thoughts come back almost instantly and they are angry at having been held down for so long.

Other people have run much further and made much less of a fuss about it. Only a child would need to pretend he was a warrior to get through such a short run. You are pathetic.

My brief respite is over and my focus once again turns to the real world, until tomorrow when I get to run again. Not really going anywhere, but somehow managing to escape all the same.

When you turn around to get off the machine, everybody will be looking at you. Men with muscles and pretty girls flushed with colour and their hair bouncing behind them will look at you with one eyebrow raised to show how unattractive you look with your shiny beetroot face and your pigeon chest.

But nobody is there when I turn around. The gym is empty, save for a giant man in the far corner lifting everything he can reach above his head and a cocky young personal trainer checking his emails on the computer by the entrance. I wipe all the evidence of my visit off the machine with the antibacterial wipes provided and head down to the shower, my legs slightly unsteady beneath me. Time to brave myself for another potential visit to the disgusting testicle buffet.

Entering the changing rooms and rounding the corner to my locker of choice:

Two for one. 241.

At first there is no one there, but as I am taking my towel from my locker and stripping down to shower (leaving my shorts on for the journey to the shower, to protect my dignity) he arrives. A sea of empty lockers to choose from and for some reason number 243 is the only choice for this short, fat man with tattoos on his arms to get ready for his swim. Most likely a prop-forward for the local rugby team, he considers his comfort with exposing his small penis to a room full of strangers to be a show of his heterosexuality.

It's my penis, deal with it. Touch it if you like, I won't be turned on 'cos I'm straight see? Touch it, go on. TOUCH IT! JUST LOOK AT IT! ASK IT SOMETHING!

I gather my things quickly and head off to the shower, selecting the one furthest from the entrance on the left-hand side. My urge is to head to the right but I avoid that as I imagine fewer people have used the left side and therefore the chance of cross-contamination is reduced. I have been lucky enough to find the shower gel I will use for the rest of my life, should market forces allow such a thing. A blend of lemon, cinnamon and coconut flavours – the lemon and coconut making

it refreshing and fragrant but the cinnamon adding a spice that justifies this as a man's product, just about.

Showering is something that I imagine everybody in the world does, eventually, the same way every day. It would be impossible over time not to get into a habit of washing the same things, in the same order, every time you execute a task. Wouldn't it? It does not come naturally to me to be spontaneous, and admittedly that is the only way in which it can come. As soon as you have planned to do something spontaneously, you actually haven't. Why wouldn't you choose to plan something ahead of time rather than 'see how it goes'? I can tell you how it will go, my friend – not as well as it would have if you had planned it.

Dressing myself after my shower, I switch my phone back on and after a moment I get two texts:

> Great. I'm off tomorrow night. Is that too soon? x

followed by:

> Good idea, I've got news about a publisher for you. Let's talk tomorrow, come to the office.

Holy shit. Now I've done it.

My whole body tingles with excitement, shivers down my spine, my scalp itches and my eyes water. Most importantly, the smile on my face is absolutely irremovable. If the man with the small penis and the tattoos comes back now I could get myself into a lot of trouble! There's no use pretending I haven't been waiting for the first text since I left Yorkshire this morning, and whatever the reason for its late arrival I can now start thinking further ahead. The pressure on a first date is absolutely immense, as memories are being stored for ever for recollection as a 'this is what we did on our first date' anecdote. Let us say, for the sake of example, that this wonderful girl and I spent a magical afternoon together walking hand in hand through a meadow, as is more than possible, but on rounding the final corner of our walk we were confronted by a huge pile of dog mess. I would berate myself unfairly for not having checked our route beforehand and removed any such offending artefacts.

Try as I might I would be unable to disassociate the thought of dog shit when I thought of her, as a truly perfect woman would never even be around such foulness. Even were we to get together and stay with one another for thirty contented years, should she turn to me one summer's evening and whisper, '*Oh Jon, do you remember our afternoon in the meadow?*' I would reply, '*Of course … There was shit everywhere!*'

As for the second text, my head's in a complete spin. I can't think about the book now – it's too much for me to take in. Besides, I have to get ready for Gemma. I would be a fool to think anything is more important than finding someone who makes me happy and who I can make happy too.

So first I need to go home and put my house back together again, then I can write a list for tomorrow and forget that this weekend ever happened. A perfect day beckons, if I can only get it right.

Planning gives me comfort in stressful times, so back at home I reach for my diary, turn to tomorrow's date and start scheduling …

MONDAY

07.58

THE PERFECT DAY BEGINS

So you've got yourself a date, says Private Jonny. *That won't come to anything.*

Well, let's just see, shall we, fights back Public Jon.

Two different people wake up in my bed each day, but they are both inside me. We are all a much more complex machine than we seem to the people who know us – I consider that I am at least two very different people.

There is the side of my personality which manifests itself most when I am with other people, the man I call 'Public Jon'. It isn't a very good nickname, rather too toiley for my tastes, but I can't think what else to call him. Despite how it may seem from what I have written about my time in shared accommodation, I actually make a lot of effort around people to be genial and pleasant company. I tell jokes almost relentlessly to attempt to amuse people. I let things go that I might otherwise have allowed to bother me and I am far more forgiving of other people than I am of myself. On a day when I am around people from morning until night, I can slowly eradicate the negative thoughts that abound at other times and by its end feel liberated and content to live as others do – a little more so anyway!

I believe strongly that you have to find happiness in your natural state. Drugs and extreme hobbies might help take you away from that natural state from time to time and this can be a very good thing, provided you are not running away from confronting life in its normal form. The things you feel when you are sober and alone cannot be outrun. When your head hits the pillow at night and there is nothing around to distract you but endless dark, that's who you are.

Friends of mine will, night after night, watch films in bed, or listen to audiobooks or music in order to help them drift off to sleep. Some people read books to achieve the same goal. In my opinion these are all ways of silencing the version of yourself that is trying to speak to you then. This is the other side of me, the one I call 'Private Jonny'. Aggressive and confrontational, he pulls no punches in making me aware of things I have done wrong that were entirely my own fault. When I get into bed tonight, I know very well that he will force me to address whatever has happened during the day.

As much as I hate him, he is the one who improves me. He reminds me of my errors so that they can be avoided in future. He makes me aware of the impact my actions had on other people, which I might have missed at the time when in what people call 'the moment'. He is important. The arguments between these two can be epic. Public Jon thinks that Private Jonny is too negative and isn't the person that defines me. He thinks that his strict rules and perfectionism are what make it harder for him to be happy around others and to find love.

Private Jonny on the other hand thinks that Public Jon is a careless hedonist, who doesn't take enough time to think through his choices and so says insensitive things and leaves people with an unfair image of who Jon really is. They both agree that too long spent discussing each other in the third person is likely to result in the evolution of a third Jon who forgets to go to the toilet and eats paper while grinning to himself quietly in the corner.

As to which of these two people is the real you, a balancing act between the two is essential. You cannot escape the latter but, do not forget, nobody else will remember that person. When you die nobody will say:

Well, Jon was a real bastard when he was around people, but alone enjoyed poetry and suffered deeply for the injustices of the world.

Wear your brightest traits on your sleeve, for all to see, and do your tailoring at home. But don't forget to

seek some happiness for yourself too. I have some very powerful memories of time spent on my own. I've eaten incredible meals on my own, travelled to beautiful places on my own but also overcome horribly difficult periods on my own, and all of those things can be important. I certainly find it difficult to relate to people who seem incapable of doing anything on their own, needing company even whilst simply watching TV and drinking a cup of tea for fear of what their brain might do to them while it has no one there to interrupt it.

The fact that Private Jonny is unhappy is down to me to change, but not now, because now he is just miserable because of the time of day.

Once I had finished getting everything back in order last night, I opened a bottle of wine as a reward, and am now paying a heavy price for having done so. Once the bottle was finished and I had indulged in a little 'Spin and Win' I felt marvellous and, I should imagine, pretty much skipped into bed. Well now I feel awful. I think I would feel absolutely fine if I had been sick the night before, but I was just drunk enough not to realise I was drunk. This is one of many pieces of logic that occurs naturally to the regular binge drinker, but will appal anyone else. The idea that a good night ends with you vomiting all that you have consumed throughout the evening to try to prevent the internal damage it will cause as you sleep should serve as a warning that those substances ought to be avoided anyway.

To me, vomiting in the evening has the power to downgrade drinking to no more than having a game of internal dress-up for adults. For one evening, I am allowed to be someone else, to speak their language and to think their thoughts, and by shedding that skin before I go to bed, I can wake up as myself again, none the worse for the experience. I am quite content to get drunk on my own, enjoying the resulting freedom to walk around my flat naked and talk to myself in a range of decreasingly accurate and increasingly racist regional accents, taking care not to develop these as a habit that might surface outside of the house.

It's not that I can't do those things sober, just that the thought doesn't really occur to me, or the risk of being caught seems too great. A neighbour redelivering a parcel once overheard me swearing at my television in a kind of Croatian–Russian hybrid accent, but then my neighbours don't like me anyway so it's not like I had anything to lose.

Despite rising at eight o'clock, I try to avoid leaving my house before nine unless absolutely essential. Travel before nine is a living hell of suits dragging unwilling bodies onto already packed buses and trains or into cars with cold seats and loud, frightfully cheerful

breakfast DJs. It is the obligation of every self-employed person in the country to alleviate some of this stress by staying at home until official working hours have begun, passing the time by drinking tea and watching breakfast news. What new global catastrophes should I feel somehow responsible for today? I have a train to catch, but not for a few hours, which is ample time to feel I could have prevented murders and berate myself for not doing more for charity. I wonder whether I feel ill simply because of the hangover, or am I nervous about how the rest of today will pan out? Decisions I make today could well affect the rest of my life – this could be the first day on a path to becoming Jon Richardson, published author and husband to Gemma, his wife and business partner in his Lakeland bistro. A smile! Now there's a turn up for the book.

12.59

TRAIN TO PADDINGTON

I can't risk going any further with Gemma. I reached this conclusion on the way to the train station. What was I thinking earlier? It wasn't really any thought in particular, but just everything. In the last two days in my head I have worshipped her, fantasised about her, stalked her – when I was sure she wasn't stalking me – called her a bitch, married her, deserted her, returned to her, nursed her in her old age and buried her – when she wasn't burying me. She has made me smash up my flat with her habit of delayed response to messages. All this craziness and I still don't even know the slightest detail about her, like if she eats meat, even if she does work in a carvery. I am certifiably insane and it's only fair that she knows that. Or maybe this is what everyone goes through when they meet someone new? Maybe she is feeling the same way about me, though I can't help but doubt it. The last time I tried to make an effort on her behalf, I ended up inventing a new scheme for not going back and checking my door, so perhaps I should do the same again today. I will try to be good natured and easy going today and maybe by our date tonight I will be a new man, a better man. There couldn't be a sterner test of my ability to be a good man than a train journey into the capital. The things that people rush around for, the jobs they cram themselves into sewers to get to, the clubs they drink in – none of them really matters beyond the M25, which encases London in its own self-interested fury. London is Dorian Gray, enjoying the excess and exuberance of its own assumed importance, while the world rots and festers somewhere upstairs in the attic.

Embarking on my journey, I try to keep focussed on what I should tolerate and what I shouldn't, what is a deliberate decision to inconvenience others and what is somebody making a mistake. Who is trying to make this situation worse and who is simply trying to get through the day? Level one – the station foyer.

In an attempt to limit the number of transactions I need to carry out which are dependent on people, I usually opt for the electronic ticket machines because the staff are capable of annoying me from the outset.

To get to the ticket booths I have to pass the display board that will inevitably tell me that the train I am here to catch is already late. I wonder constantly whether I moan too much or whether things really are just not good enough. There are people whose lives are much worse than mine, but is there really anyone in this country who never gets annoyed at late trains or litter because things could be worse? I doubt it. I am very aware that I could not hope to run a national rail service myself and so I try hard not to let minor delays bother me, but when ticket prices go up and punctuality goes down, it is difficult to maintain rationality. Fantasy retribution is all one can trust in at times.

Worse still is the fact that apologies are meted out by robotic pre-recorded voices, as so many need to be made that to employ a real person to apologise each time a service is delayed would cost thousands and would drain so much sincerity out of that person that by the time they got home they would be unable to summon any emotion even if they were to find their house had been burnt to the ground. They would simply comment that it had happened and start on their way into alternative accommodation, incapable of feeling sorry for themselves or anyone any more.

So instead, Johnny 5 waits by the public address system, ready to update customers on the fact that the 1347 Bristol Temple Meads service is stuck behind a slower-moving freight service that managed to get onto the tracks without any of the people who control the lines wondering what impact that might have on scheduled services which people have paid not insubstantial amounts of money to board.

I. Am. Sorry … For. The. In.convenience. This. Will. Cause. You.

No you are not, you are a robot, and if the cinema of the 1980s has taught us nothing else, it has taught us that robots cannot feel human emotions.

What. Is. Love? What. Is. RailReplacementBusService?

It is this very lack of emotion that makes me love computers, because there is always a reason for their malfunction – provided you don't fall into the trap of thinking that the machines you use care about you, by which I mean you do not ask your computer why it is going so slowly, do not joke that it doesn't like Monday mornings and absolutely do not give your car a name.

Anyone who responds to a question about where to put an item from a draining board with a comment like 'The colander lives in that cupboard there' needs help. Colanders and tin openers do not live anywhere; they do not live at all. They do not choose to let you down; they simply break. Machines break and that is a fact and if you waste your time thinking that this is part of some wider scheme then you are never going to get through the day and you will never achieve what you could. Now if *you* were to break your tin opener through misuse or lose it through carelessness then that is a different matter. People live – save your emotion for them.

The fast ticket machine therefore offers a wonderful chance to collect one's ticket without having to confront

another person who might be upset or grumpy or might just take a dislike to your face or necktie that makes them want to serve you poorly. Or so it should be, until you are unfortunate enough to join a queue which has formed behind someone who has clearly not only never used a fast ticket machine before, but has never used any piece of equipment invented after 1950, as I just have.

Some people have an awesome skill for remaining oblivious to the fact that they are in the way, as if they see their peripheral vision as an optional extra to their tunnel vision, to be saved for best and not worn out when not needed.

Don't get me wrong, I can find myself in the way as well as anybody on the planet, but as with so many problems, admitting that you are a sufferer is half the battle. I have learned over time that should I need to abandon my trolley whilst shopping to run back for a forgotten bulb of garlic, then you can be sure that whatever I park it in front of will suddenly be required by somebody. Even if I park my wagon adjacent to the shelf containing dolphin-unfriendly tuna chunks pickled in their own piss, then within moments there will be a run on them by every shopper in a two-hundred-metre radius.

I'm so good at stimulating interest in a product that I should be paid by the supermarkets to help them shift slower lines. All this said, I do what I can to minimise

the effect my condition has on others by leaving my trolley somewhere as inconspicuous as possible and by returning to it as quickly as possible, apologising if I can see I have inconvenienced anyone in the process.

The man I am now watching attempt to extract his train ticket from a machine he does not understand is the train-station equivalent of two people having a tedious conversation in the middle of a shopping aisle with their trolleys side by side, at right angles to the shelving like a police roadblock.

Sorry you can't get to the baked beans right now – there has been an incident ahead and I'm gathering evidence from Maggie here about Len's vasectomy.

I am wondering why the person behind him doesn't step forward to offer assistance when it becomes clear that he is already seeking help from whomever he is talking to on the phone. Proving my theory that relationships serve only to halve the responsibility people take for themselves, he has called his wife to see if she can help with the predicament in which he now finds himself. How a man so incompetent finds a partner I will never know but I mustn't be sexist, as women are equally capable of incompetence as men so they may well prove to be two identically inept peas in a festering pod of ignorance.

Annoyed, I decide to brave the desk after all and regret my earlier judgement. The lady who serves me is polite, smiles broadly and is as efficient as I could have hoped for. She wishes me a safe journey and unwittingly guilt-trips me into wanting to go and apologise to the man at the ticket machine for the horrible thoughts I had about him, no doubt a result of my own internal frustrations.

When I turn to go through the gate, that man is still on the phone to his wife, who is probably shouting random numbers and letters into the ear of a husband I am sure she hoped to have an afternoon without. Having painted him as a cartoon villain I now see into the eyes set deep into his face, beneath a pair of heavy, tired eyebrows. His eyes look startled and afraid, the eyes of a great ape who has only ever known life in a cage, meals provided and medical intervention in case of illness, who has then been thrown out on to the busy street to fend for himself – it isn't that he is unaware that he is in the way at all, he is simply absolutely unsure of everything.

His mind is screaming at him in a language he doesn't speak and he looks as though all he wants to do is crawl into a corner of the ticket hall and suck his thumb. Still I cannot help but think that if he didn't have a wife he would have been forced to address the need to fend for himself before now, but in thinking that I realise I am jealous more than anything else. I am not oblivious to the fact that his fate will befall me

sooner or later and I will reach an age at which no one would ever believe that it was once me who was in a rush to get somewhere.

I used to have meetings you know! In London and everything! is what I will cry to the people who rush by me on either side, tutting their disgust at my continued existence.

Whatever, granddad – go back to sleep.

I might have a chance at being a granddad now after all, just maybe. But don't get too far ahead of yourself – she will think that odd. Just concentrate on today, get the things right that you can and allow the rest of your life to click easily into place.

50004. 0000000000004. 4GOTTEN.

Private Jonny is starting to whisper inside my head.

Do you think that book you want to write about not having a girlfriend and being a compulsive weirdo is going to change things for the better, or are you nailing shut your own coffin? Talk to me!

I look up at the display and check which platform I need: platform 3, which is along the tunnel that goes under the track and then up the stairs on the right. Most people follow the signs leading to the left but experience has taught me that heading right avoids the crowds and brings me out closer to where the quiet carriage will be when the train arrives. One nil to me.

I have long thought that the problem with public transport is that there is far too much of the former doing far too little of the latter, and once on the train this proves to be exactly the case. My carriage is typical of most on the train in that it is full (except up in first class, of course, where money buys you dignity not afforded to the urchins who paid a meagre fifty pounds for their ticket; we get what we deserve). Not quite full to standing, or I might have felt pressure to stand myself, but with all seats taken.

Although the grammatically execrable train manager's announcement makes it clear that this is the quiet carriage, somehow there appears to be an unwritten agreement that the rules no longer apply once the train is so busy that people are forced to sit here who might ordinarily have been sat elsewhere. This makes absolutely no difference as far as I am concerned. Just as most decent people stop to put on trousers before running out of a hotel in the case of a fire alarm because the rules of decency that apply in society take precedence over the inconvenience – people would rather die than expose their genitals to a stranger – so here, the quiet carriage remains the quiet carriage, whatever your reason for being inside it. The noise in this carriage is certainly no worse than in any other carriage, but the stickers on the wall remind us of the fact that this should be a haven, and serve only to

further frustrate those of us who are obeying the rules, in much the same way that a speed limit sign warning you not to exceed 50 mph is an infuriating tease when you're sat motionless in traffic.

In spite of all this, the young man next to me – wearing a smart grey suit but with a piercing through his lower lip and his hair infuriatingly flopping down over one eye, as if using two is some sort of conformist weakness – is listening to what I suppose he considers to be music. I am having the thoughts of a man thrice my actual age, but what difference does it make if they are the right ones?

In the fantasy inside my head I pull his headphones out from his ears and lean menacingly into him, whispering:

Listen to me, you ignorant little piece of shit, turn your fucking music down and listen to the voice inside your head. This rap music you are listening to makes you believe that you are oppressed and beaten down and capable of so much more if only 'they' would let you express yourself, but 'they' do not exist. Whatever shitty little job you do in your shitty little suit is part of it, the little packed lunch you have in your bag down there is part of it and the rules of this carriage on the train are part of it. 'They' are us, we are them and if you really hate society then go and live in a fucking cave by the sea, but if you want to earn money and ride on

trains and eat at McDonald's then you are a fucking part of it.

I don't say anything, though. I just rehearse the speech over and over in my head and it escalates with each repetition and grows more and more violent until five minutes into the journey I am imagining myself tapping him on the shoulder, then as he turns around I grab his face in the palm of my hand and drive his head backwards through the window. The severity of this image shocks even me and I shudder slightly at the thought of it. He is probably not much older than twenty and even if it takes him another twenty years to learn to behave better then he will be a positive influence on the planet for another forty years. Right now he is just someone stuck in a job he hates listening to some music. Calm down, Jon.

But I'm tired of calming myself down. Isn't it the case that if his music weren't too loud then I wouldn't have been angry in the first place. I can rationalise it all I like but I am suffering at the hands of people behaving less well than myself. I have heard people arguing with ticket inspectors enforcing the quiet carriage's rules that the sound of a person talking on their phone is no louder than two people having a conversation, but that really isn't the point.

Aside from how annoying it is having to listen to half a conversation and piece together the rest, the fact

remains that the use of mobile phones is forbidden. I can't stand being around people who challenge every rule on principle because they think it makes them a more interesting person. We do not live in a dictatorship, your civil liberties are not at risk and rules are in place to protect not punish the majority of us; however much of a square it makes me I don't see why we can't just assume that rules are in place for a reason and follow them silently until given a valid reason to do otherwise. I won't bring kids into a world where people act so defiantly in their own self-interest.

If the sign says using your phone may interfere with equipment then maybe it does; if the pilot says keep your seatbelt on until the plane has come to a complete halt then keep your fucking seatbelt on! I will die a happy man if just once I am on a plane that *is* forced to stop suddenly on the runway and all the cocky business twats and pig-faced holidaymakers who had to get up and stretch their varicose-vein-ridden legs are thrown forward into a big pile of broken bones and flesh because they know which rules apply to them and which are here to keep them down.

Many people are listening to loud music or talking on their phones – someone went first and nobody spoke up so now several have followed. There is one man I can see at a table further down the aisle who I am just itching to hate more than the others. I know for a fact

that he is, over and above his phone conversation, a total penis; I just can't work out exactly why just yet. My rage-dar is drawn to him nonetheless and is beeping like crazy.

There *is* something definitely worse about this man than all the others, something other than the fact he has sunglasses on top of his head inside on a clearly dark and dank afternoon. Something in his eyes tells me that he feels as if he is superior to all of us and the drama he expresses during his conversation is clearly a performance mostly for our benefit.

The way he keeps rubbing his eyes as if in slow motion in the midst of his conversation is particularly annoying. It is the sort of thumb and two-finger pinching towards the bridge of the nose action that put upon police chiefs use in films like *Beverly Hills Cop* and is clearly an entirely learned mannerism. There is no natural instinct to do this, it serves no purpose, but is merely something that people see in films and subconsciously decide to do in public so that everyone around can be made aware of how put upon they are by the constant dithering of the morons they have been put in charge of. I think cinema has made us all act out the drama in our lives far more than we used to in the days before there was a television in every house.

The default position for the human face is pretty much blank, eyes fixed on a point somewhere in the

distance, mouth slightly ajar but still and eyebrows unmoving. This is never shown in films though because in films something must always be happening, actors are paid to act or react to whatever drama is unfolding and so we are much more accustomed to seeing eyebrows raised or furrowed, nostrils pinched together and mouths open with shock. We crave a sense that we are somehow important and in a bid to make our own lives feel noteworthy we react in a similar way to the news in the coffee shop that there are no more ginger biscuits, rather than accept that this is an almost irrelevant piece of news.

I remember as a child I used to skip a little before I started running because I had seen people doing it in films. Rather than just set off running, I would look over my left shoulder, look at my watch, do a little skip and then run. I suppose I thought it made you run faster and look cooler. It didn't and I grew out of it.

It's not true that you shouldn't judge a book by its cover, since that is precisely why covers are put on books, to allow you to better understand the contents without going to the bother of reading them in their entirety. If this man were a book he would be called *An Idiot's Guide to Acting like a Total Wanker in Mundane Situations*.

It probably doesn't help that the man on his phone is good looking, and clearly wearing a very expensive

suit, though I can't help but think to myself that if he were that important he wouldn't be squashed into a standard-class carriage, would he? Important people don't have to rush or get stressed, because the things they are on their way to wait for them. This show of stress is for our benefit, not his, but people are buying it.

I think the same when I see people speeding through rough areas of shit-hole towns; what meeting could someone driving a lowered Vauxhall Nova with what looks like a catering-size tin of beans for an exhaust possibly be late for in a dump like this? Don't want to miss the McDonald's breakfast? People speed to convince themselves that their lives are of some sort of significance and people overdress for the same reason. It's safe to say that despite never having spoken to him and not knowing so much as his first name, I hate him. Never mind the new effort I am supposed to be making to be a better person for Gemma or for anyone else, this man is a wanker and it seems that up to now only I know it.

Looking around for new targets, I realise it isn't all bad on the train. I overhear one woman shouting down her handset, 'What? WHAT? Well then, what I suggest you do, *Michael*, is just put cling film over it and I'll bloody well eat it when I get back!' So perhaps not all the conversations here are about global trade deals or matters of international security as they seemed. Her

irrational anger mirrors my own and makes me smile. I wonder if I could divert so much energy into liking people for no reason as I do to hating them?

As I smile I notice a girl sat next to Sunglasses McWankerpants looking over at me. She isn't smiling at me though, and when I look away and look back again she is still looking. My smile fades as flirting decorum indicates that it is necessary to look brooding and angry so that prospective mates can see how deep and thoughtful you are. Which film did we get this idea from? A few more pauses and a few more glances later and she is looking back most of the time.

Could she be looking at me? Are we beginning a flirtatious period? Am I going to cheat on Gemma already? (OK, I've already cheated on her in my mind, but this could be for real, even if we haven't even started on a relationship yet.) How could I do that to either of them? I'm already a potential two-timer. What kind of sleazy scumbag am I? And anyway, it's not as if I'm even any good at flirting.

Now I break out into a nervous sweat as this is the realm in which I am least comfortable. Flirting is all about showing yourself in the best light possible, moving in a sexy way, holding yourself together and appearing sexy – not easy. In truth this is the stage I would rather cut out altogether from the whole dating process. Humans should be forced to carry around with them a laminated list of everything they are good and bad at, in order, which they can then hand to anyone who shows interest in them.

'Here are my details. Check the good list there and you will see cooking – that's right I used to be a chef – keeping fit, my attentiveness rating is high and I have a decent score for generosity. If you just turn the list over, OK, now just there in between fixing my own car and touching spiders with my bare hands you'll see staying up all night banging women senseless and doing drugs on a weeknight – not me I'm afraid. Anyway, have a good long look at the list and if that looks like a trade-off you are happy to make then give me a call.'

I'm not a stud and I do not do sexy chat – I do awkward jokes that are endearing to begin with in a Hugh-Grant-kind-of-a-way, but grow ever more irritating and soon become an obvious attempt to avoid any genuinely open conversation about emotions. If a woman leaned over to me on a train and said, 'I'm not wearing any knickers', I know for a fact I would not be able to help myself from replying with, 'Me neither – don't you find that boxer shorts help your testicles breathe?'

I can't actually be sure whether she is looking over at me romantically, as I am at her, or if she is simply trying to work out why the pointy-featured weirdo is staring

so intently at her with his occasional manic smile. I try to remember what the smile I did earlier looked like, in case she saw me do it, and without thinking try to re-enact it. It comes out all wrong, as my eyebrows are furrowed with concentration and the smile uses too many of the muscles in my face. I imagine I look like a baby making a deliberate effort to soil its pants. If she saw that then she will definitely think I am a nutcase.

This is a trap into which I fall regularly on public transport, believing that the girl I am seated opposite is falling in love with me, rather than the truth which is that she is probably just growing increasingly frightened of the lecherous pervert smirking at her over the top of his newspaper. Right now this girl seems perfect, attractive and well dressed and conforming to all the rules of her chosen carriage – hell yeah, you abide by those guidelines, you kinky little mare!

Shall we have sex outside in this field? Not without the expressed written permission of the landowner!

This thought again makes me smile, for the second time in as many minutes, and the smile feels oddly out of place. I wonder why? Somehow it feels inappropriate, as if I have started smirking at a funeral, and then I remember that I was occupying my mind with hating people. What a ridiculous state of affairs, that a moment's fun should feel a distraction from my stated mission of boiling myself to the point of internal combustion with ire. Hate feels productive to me, as if by noticing the problems in the world I am helping to make it better.

Children are just about the only group of people widely accepted as a staple of comedic hatred that I like. Impulsive and energetic entirely by nature rather than vain denial of the truth, they laugh and cry and are the only people on the planet who live in the moment, not because they stubbornly refuse to think of anything else, but because they genuinely don't know it exists.

I envy them that. I remember a time in my own life when I lived simply to 'play out', ate meals that weren't planned ahead that morning and fell because I was so eager to get to new places. I place my steps now for fear of looking foolish and my greatest fear is that a child of my own, subjected to too much of my company, would pick up on that side of me and I would deprive someone precious of a chance to live properly. No child should have to suffer a father like me, nor even a babysitter like me.

If I were Mary Poppins my songs would be about how carefully I have to pack my bag because magical, bottomless ones don't really exist, or about how those who need sugar to take their medicine need to grow up and start acting like adults or they will get fat. What

hope could I have of raising a balanced child? And if I accept that I could not, then planning for a relationship that might lead to such an eventuality is like premeditated child abuse. I resolve not to look at the girl any more and to be upfront with Gemma at our dinner tonight about all of this. What better end could there be to our Brief Encounter?

While I have been fantasising about how miserable I could make this stranger and our unborn offspring, the train has slowed down to a gradual halt. Even the creature next to me has taken off its headphones in anticipation of an announcement explaining the delay. This only means that the music now is even louder and I can identify certain lyrics as well as the drums. Something about bitches and what they be all like. And then something about haters. Sing it! I guess he's talking about people like me.

'Come on, for God's sake!' someone shouts, pointlessly.

I don't think we have stopped because the driver feels we have lost our enthusiasm for the journey, but I suppose someone had to try something. All around the train phone conversations are finally coming to an end and the carriage is growing more and more quiet. I love the expression on the faces of those who have been talking non-stop on phones since we left Swindon. You don't have to drive into the

countryside and sit alone for hours on a rock to experience a sense of complete isolation – I often think the people who are most acutely aware of their spiritual solitude are commuters on trains who lose signal on their mobile phones in the middle of a conversation.

Where just moments before they were ignorant of all the people around them, shouting and laughing into their handset, they are now (after a few obligatory 'hello?'s) staring around the train compartment, working out whether or not they have upset anyone or shared personal details at too high a volume. They will then fiddle with their phone, or get papers out of their briefcases, anything to avoid facing up to the nothingness. Mobile phones have robbed people of the feeling of ever being alone, much to their detriment I fear. Company pollutes the mind.

It is a few more minutes before the train manager announces the reason for the hold-up to the stranded passengers, which he does over the tinny and slightly too quiet public-address system, a problem made worse by his nasal and stilted vocal style, as he manages miraculously not to place the emphasis at the correct point on any of the words he wrestles into submission.

'Ladies an'gennlemen, this is your train manager speakin'. We would like to apologise for the delay in your journey today. We are currently bein' held just

251

aarside Readin' Station aaaand this is due. To a suicidal trespasser on the tracks. Once again we apologise-forthedelay and any inconvenience this will cause to you today. Thanyou. Meh.'

The phrase 'suicidal trespasser' makes me feel sick with disgust. What a cold and clinical term to describe someone whose life has collapsed completely around them. It is not yet three o'clock in the afternoon and already someone has found themselves so despairing of life that they are contemplating suicide, and all they represent to those working for the train company is a legal inconvenience.

At four o'clock this morning that person was some-one who was too depressed to sleep, at seven o'clock they were probably in tears and starting to drink and by now they are in search of the most permanent answer there is to what might have been a problem with many alternative solutions. At what point in deciding to kill yourself does trespass cease to be an issue? After you are dead?

'Ladies and gentleman, we apologise for the delay but this is due to a very naughty trespassing corpse lying under a good, honest, hard-working train in the Waterloo area.'

For most of us on the train, to be fair, this is at least sufficient reason to accept our lot and stop complaining, some perhaps taking a moment to reflect on how

lucky we are to have jobs worth commuting to and others resolving to phone loved ones when they eventually make it home. What stuns me beyond all previous levels of disgust with the world is that for some people this serves only as an excuse to grow even more impatient. Not only does there seem to be no sense of tragedy about this for them, no suggestion that we all get out to try and help as we might if someone in front of us had fallen off a bridge or crashed their car, but instead it is an annoyance.

Well! Leaves on the track I could understand, but this? Honestly! Why don't the police step in and stop these people?

How could people really be so heartless? So willing to look after number one in the face of any challenge? Of course, chief amongst these heartless hecklers is eye-pinching Terminator, who I overhear say to the person he is speaking to, 'Oh for God's sake! Look, Martin, you're going to have to call Nigel and tell him I'm going to be late. Some fucking idiot is trying to throw himself under the train so I'm probably going to miss my connection. Selfish arsehole! Look, can you call Nigel and then call me straight back and let me know what he says?'

I sit utterly speechless – not that I would have had anyone to speak to even if I had wanted to say something; in my head the guy next to me is a mess of blood

and broken glass. I suspect he isn't alone in what he is thinking, but most other people at least have enough of a sense of decency to keep their self-interested concerns to themselves. Were I less of a coward I might have challenged him directly, but fortunately a less danger-ous opportunity for vengeance is presenting itself, one that I cannot turn down.

'Oh, wait, Martin, are you still there? Right, this piece of shit phone is about to die so you'll have to call me on my private number. Have you got a pen?'

Not missing the irony of this man's lament for the death of his mobile-phone battery, which he seems to care for more than another human being, I spot my chance and reach for my own phone, typing the numbers in as he dictates them.

'Ok, yeah. It's 0 ... 7...'

The pause between the 0 and the 7 is further evidence, as if any were needed, that this guy is a total dick. What mobile number doesn't start with 07? Does he need to patronise Martin like this, or is Martin really stupid enough to reply with '07? Hang on! That's the same as your work number, are you sure you're giving me the right one?'

By the time he has finished speaking I have his whole number stored in my phone, helpfully repeated back by the unsuspecting egotist, and now all I have to

decide is exactly what I am going to do with it. Will I wait until later and call him up from a payphone somewhere? Might I leave the number around various public toilets and phone boxes in London? Probably not, since this would involve a need for graffiti and therefore the loss of my moral high ground. I feel as though I need to act straight away, to make amends for so many missed opportunities in the past, so I carpe the diem good and proper, click 'Compose Message' and begin to type.

> Dear Arrogant Business Twat. Please note that no one else in the QUIET carriage gives a shit about your tedious existence, take your call elsewhere. Yours, Everyone In Carriage A (the QUIET carriage) P.S. You look like a cock in those sunglasses.

I send the message to the number I have written down in my address book, await the screen that informs me that my message has been sent safely and switch off my phone, making me untraceable. I am no longer the sender of the message, I am part of a carriage of law-abiding citizens. Greysuit and I are now team-mates

along with Sexy Girl and Microwave Dinners. Our name is Legion.

I see the message arrive at his phone a moment later and am caught between my urge to see the result and my desire not to get caught. I decide he can't look at me and read the message so I look over furtively. He reads it silently, before eyeing everyone in the carriage suspiciously. It crosses my mind that I might have made things worse: if he decides to react angrily someone who has done nothing wrong might be inconvenienced, but thankfully save for a sarcastic cry of 'Well done!' he doesn't seem to react much at all, until his face grows red.

There is a scrap of decency inside you, isn't there? I think. Show love for the haters – sometime we win one back. Before he can do anything much more his phone rings and the news comes back from Martin about his delayed meeting. I can't hear whether or not Nigel was able to reschedule as the subsequent chat is too quiet for me to hear. Mission accomplished, although frustratingly I now feel an annoying lack of closure about a story unfinished. If I go over and ask whether or not the meeting is still on he will definitely know it was me who sent the message, but I can't help but want to know. Oh well. I allow myself a smirk of celebration, which if I had seen it on anyone's face but my own, I would have hated beyond belief.

I also never get to hear what happens to the trespasser, as five minutes later the train pulls into Reading
station and no more is said of the matter, but the tone
of the journey is different after that, for me at least. I
start to get nervous about arriving in London and all
that it entails. Aside from the importance of the meeting I am so ill-prepared for, for an organiser like myself,
a journey across London must be planned with military
precision.

London is not the kind of city you simply drift around.
If you do not have a plan then it will eat you up and
before you know it you are simply wandering around
in the rain, exhausted and wishing you were anywhere else as people shove past you in order to
make you aware of just how important they are
and what a rush they are in to get where they need
to be.

The underground is manageable outside of rush
hour. The underground map is an absolute work of art,
breaking London down as it does to a series of coloured
lines with dots on. There is no crime, there are no
people or buildings or pigeons, just a fractured rainbow of possible destinations. It all seems so simple
down here, like Tron, all straight lines and clear
options. Down here there is nothing between Oxford

Circus and Piccadilly or Tottenham Court Road, but up there are obstacles and wrong turnings.

When I come out of the underground station it is raining and overcast and I have half a mile or so to cover on foot. The rain will thin out the number of people on the streets I suppose, but means I won't be able to get my phone out to check my route on its screen, although the frightened fifteen-year-old northerner in me knows that if I do that then I will become a victim of crime quicker than you can say Dick Van Dyke anyway.

A typical journey on foot through London will find me imagining the horrific murders of anything upwards of five complete strangers. First in line today is the young man who spits on the floor right outside the station exit through which I have just come after negotiating the ticket gate first time and thus avoiding death by stampede. I don't mean to suggest that he aimed his spit maliciously to inconvenience me specifically, since I am almost certain he doesn't even know I exist. He was just spitting aimlessly, for want of anything better to do at that moment in time.

When is the last time I spewed my bacteria-ridden innards down onto the pavement for someone to step in and traipse through their house? Can't remember ... Best do one now to be on the safe side.

For him I picture a cartoon rain cloud over his head, which follows him wherever he runs *à la Tom and Jerry*, but a cloud which rains down acid which slowly eats away at the fabric of his clothing and then his skin and bones. Just my little secret.

15.00

MEETING IN LONDON RE: BOOK

Usually when I have to go to meetings in London I am
annoyed that all this stress will be for nothing since I
generally know how the next hour will pan out. Nothing
of any importance normally happens in meeting rooms
in London or any other city for that matter, we all just
meet up to play the game and feel as though we have
earned a glass of wine with our dinner that evening and
have stories to tell our partners. Meeting chat can be
boiled down succinctly to:

'Are you still doing stuff?'

'Yeah, I'm still doing stuff. You doing stuff?'

'Oh yeah. I started stuff early this morning and will
be doing stuff until late tonight. I hope the stuff goes
well because then things will happen.'

'Without doubt. The whole team agree that the
occurrence of things as a result of stuff is inevitable.
Ours is not to question, right!'

'Too right. OK. If that's all I have to stare at a screen
for a period now, then take a call from a person.'

'OK. Bye.'

Handshakes will follow, and possibly awkward hugs given that the lines between formality and friendship have been blurred by our pretence of banter. Do I shake a man's hand but kiss a woman or do I shake everybody's hand? If I kiss a woman then am I not sexualising a business occasion and therefore subconsciously undermining it? How many times do I meet a man before we do an awkward lean-in and touch shoulders handshake? Is a high five a suitable end to a meeting? So many questions!

The meeting will almost always be fine and as usual the people involved will all agree that if we were to make something really good, then that would be good. No one will know what the thing should be or how we go about making it, but the consensus will be that good things can happen and are good. At times like this I try to repress my cynicism but it's so hard to have any confidence in what you are doing in a city so large.

But today's different. For a start my agent is here at the meeting, and I never see my agent – I don't mean 'I never usually see my agent', I mean 'I have *never before seen* my agent.' We generally communicate, if at all, by phone, email, text and of course post, with my fees clearly billed minus expenses and agency percentage. Yet here he is – I know it's him because I once saw a photo – along with some people from the publisher – a

director of some sort and an editor, a publicist and a couple more suits. Everyone's beaming, hands are shaken, coffees all round.

'And the idea is that you're single – and your … personality issues … make it impossible for you to form lasting relationships?'

'Mmm, can't get a girlfriend for love or money.'

'Love it. Crippling self-doubt, is it?'

'Haha. Sure.'

'And of course it will obviously be a very funny book – just like your stand-up …?'

'Well, yes, though it does have its serious side –'

'But the book will be funny?'

'Hilarious.'

'Well, I think that's all we need to know. We've got a contract ready for you to sign … Jasper?'

'I have it here, Toby.'

The contract is handed to me.

I almost start to write the name *Gemma*, then quickly change the G to a J and hope that no one has noticed.

G for Gemma.

J for Jon … and of course for Judas.

★ ★ ★

Back out onto the streets, future jeopardised, career secured.

I have certainly achieved a lot in my twenties, but at what cost? I mean everything that I say when I say it, but then I look back and wonder how I became who I am.

This is the place to be if you feel insecure about what you are, since nothing is real here in London. It is as if everyone out in the streets has agreed to frown and move quickly to cover up the fact that no one quite knows how we ended up this way. No sooner have I exited the building than I am already getting in the way of people far busier and more important than myself hurrying along the bustling Soho street on which I find myself.

In order not to annoy anybody else I pick a direction and start walking in it, quickly. I'm not sure whether this is the way to where I need to be or not but if I turn around abruptly there will be a pile-up of hundreds of people which could threaten to kill dozens of innocent men, women and children. Or so it seems.

I should stop and make sure I am heading in the right direction but I don't. If I keep on walking then eventually I am bound to end up somewhere – this feels right to me. What are all these people doing? How can there be so many of them? If London is the capital of the United Kingdom then how is it functioning with this

many people not in offices doing work? There are just so many people and I am starting to feel a little claustrophobic. I wish I was back at home but I can't just click my fingers and be there; in fact I doubt I could even try without looking absolutely insane. They don't make ruby slippers for the modern man, more to the pity.

Next on my imaginary death row, following in the footsteps of the spitter, is a heavy-set, crop-haired man, all alone in a brand-new Jeep Cherokee, stranded in a bottleneck in the road and unable for legal reasons to off-road his way out of trouble through the front of Marks & Spencer, down the escalators from lingerie to homewares, past gentlemen's slacks and out of its rear entrance, as befits a human piece of shit. All he knows for sure is that he is in a queue of at least seven cars, but it is impossible to tell for sure how far this tailback reaches as the jam stretches out at least to the end of the road and then off into obscurity as the road sweeps to the left.

What is clear to this man, however, as he smokes a cigarette and leans out of his window to get a better view of what he can already see from inside the car, is that of all the people waiting it is he who is inconvenienced the most. He can tell this because nobody else is doing anything to ameliorate the situation. No acceptance of fate for him, not in such a big important

machine, for he has finally worked out that traffic jams only exist because nobody has thought to blast their horn at one before.

The leader of the pack, in his superior tank of a vehicle, need only assert his dominance and the cars ahead will dissipate like so many terrified mice. I cannot help but wonder if any part of him honestly believed that after a long, deep belch of his horn the person at the front of the queue might be jolted into the realisation that they actually could have moved forward hours ago. I suspect not.

He hasn't tried swearing yet but I won't be around to hear phase two, though I am certain it will follow as surely as cold, frosty night follows drab, rainy day. A meteor strike for him, driving his body down and down into the bowels of the earth in a mess of flames, rock fragments and twisted metal. Very creative.

Then I see something that makes my entire day take a complete U-turn, just the kind I need to head in what I am now sure would be the right direction! A dippy-looking moron in a pork-pie hat with big hair sticking out from all sides of it, wearing skinny jeans that are neither wide enough nor long enough for his wiry frame and a green vest despite the appalling conditions, drifts out of a McDonald's, holding a small brown bag, the kind hobos drink from in American movies, save for the corporate logo on the side.

He catches my attention primarily because he fails to hold the door for the child running merrily behind him, whose infectiously radiant, gap-toothed grin proves that whatever other crimes McDonald's may be guilty of, falsely advertising their 'Happy Meals' is not one of them.

This flouncing wastrel focusses immediately on greedily extricating a paper-wrapped burger from his goody bag, which he tosses into the wind, Mother Nature's street sweeper. In his haste, he inexplicably seems to be tearing at the wrapping with both hands and by the time he realises that he has failed to allot any of his digits to the task of holding on to the burger itself, it is already too late. The golden, sesame-seed-coated bun is free and seems to fall in slow motion, performing a neatly tucked triple pike with toe loop, before hitting the ground with an immensely satisfying *thud*.

For a moment or two our man simply stands frozen to the spot as if still struggling to come to terms with the physics of what just happened, then he slowly removes his thick-rimmed eighties NHS-style glasses without altering his gaze, the way people do in films to deliver a blood-curdling death threat with full eye-contact to their sworn enemies, and stares down at what thirty seconds ago was his dinner, which now looks like hideous roadkill, ketchup and mayonnaise

arcing out like blood and guts into the road from the impact.

He looks pathetic now, all the arrogance faded but sure to return as quickly as it left. Because I know it could so easily have been me (but mainly because he was wearing a stupid hat) I start laughing and do not stop – in fact getting louder and louder – until I arrive back at the underground station some fifteen minutes later, ending up in the right place as much by luck as good judgement.

These are truly the precious moments and simply recalling this memory later as I try to sleep will, I know very well, provide me with ten more minutes of glorious, uproarious laughter.

I once read that there are three types of laughter. The first is laughter at someone else's expense – this is the laugh you do when someone walks into a flawlessly polished glass door at the supermarket and spills their shopping all over the floor – which is *very* unhealthy in terms of your inner psychological balance.

The second kind of laughter is that which comes at your own expense – this is a laugh which might accompany the phrase, 'I'm such an arsehole sometimes!' as the realisation hits you that you have been unable to find your glasses anywhere in the house simply because you are wearing them to facilitate a more accurate search – this is *mildly* unhealthy.

The third and final type of laughter, the *healthy* kind, comes at no one's expense at all, and I genuinely cannot think of a single example of how this might come to be. Perhaps there are people out there who are able to drive themselves to the point of incontinence by looking at a spoon, or thinking of the word 'bumbag', but I can't claim to have met one. If I did, I would probably laugh at how simple they were, which would make them a laugh-type one enabler and no different to a heroin dealer in my eyes.

If I didn't laugh at the misfortunes that befell other people, then there would be only tragedy and injustice, and with them a life not worth living. I have spent long enough not laughing. Despite the laughter I am already desperate to leave this city and never speak to anyone again. This extreme probably won't be necessary, but coming to London has served one purpose in that it has made me miss the sanctuary of Swindon. I want to go home. Then I remember that home is no longer a place of sanctuary, home is where I have to start getting ready for my evening with Gemma.

17.48

MY DINNER WITH GEMMA

Perhaps I will go to dinner with Gemma and then cancel the book deal in the morning. Even if it turns out to be a mistake it will have been made with good intentions and I can stop doubting myself. I want to believe that she is the one because I want to believe that there was a reason I have waited eight years, a story to tell our grandchildren, but she probably isn't. Life doesn't work like that. I read an article recently about a separated father and daughter who reunited and then fell in love with one another. 'We're soulmates,' the caption read beneath a picture dominated by his smiling face and her pregnant belly. *No you aren't*, I thought, *there's no such thing*. Like all ideas, the idea of soulmates was created at a time when the world wasn't so big. Religion prospered when it didn't have to deal with multiculturalism, now it is drowning.

Staring at my face in the bathroom mirror I cannot help but pull faces at myself. It starts when I raise my eyebrows to see how wrinkled my forehead is becoming, which I can never do without contorting the rest of my face into an expression of mock surprise, something like Edvard Munch's *The Scream*. The lines I have are there to stay, obviously, but they seem to be growing deeper at an unfair rate. I am not a particularly vain person but it seems unfair that someone who cannot step on a crack in the pavement without shuddering slightly should have to confront a future with several of them etched deep into his own face.

Then I scrunch up my eyes and nose like an angry rabbit to note the damage that time is doing to these areas and by now the gate is blown wide open and madness rushes out into the world. Sticking my tongue out, blowing up my cheeks, pulling out my ears, I do it all, never breaking a smile because I have seen it all so many times, until I start to brush my teeth. Even here the ritual includes a sketch in which I hold the paste-laden toothbrush firm in my hands and move my head around it to get the job done. It's not that I still find it funny, just that like so many things I can't stop doing it. Brushing my teeth is good thinking time because, like anything you have to do twice a day, I have my technique down to a fine art allowing my mind to wander free.

Only two hours ago I signed a contract to write a book about the impossibility of my having any kind of relationship, lasting or otherwise, and in just a couple

more hours Gemma and I will be on our first date. I haven't yet sorted out a restaurant, since the short notice means we will be just 'playing it by ear', though I would be much more comfortable had we been able to book a table somewhere. I would go so far as to say that I would prefer to know in advance the restaurant we will be going to, so that I can look at the menu online and even decide what I will order in advance. This will help me to look like I know what I want when we get there and more importantly will eliminate any possible errors.

Yes, of course some of the excitement will have gone also, but this is a price I am willing to pay. Meal mistakes include not ordering enough food and feeling agitated for the rest of evening, ordering something which might lead to later problems (bad breath, upset stomach and so on) or, worst of all, ordering something you do not like. There is a pressure to look as if you know a lot about food on a date and to show a willingness to try new things – this should be avoided at all costs!

The last time I took a girl to dinner she ordered something flamboyant and subsequently spent the rest of the meal picking at it with a fork and looking over sadly towards my own flawless, if slightly less swashbuckling, selection. Maybe she thought I would offer to share with her. Whoops, hungry *and* wrong!

That was a date which came about as a result of my being a comedian, something I learned very early on to avoid. People who find me attractive as a result of what I do for a living are to be avoided at all costs, in order to perpetuate their affection for me. When all someone has seen of you is a powerful and confident twenty-minute précis of your life, with all the boring bits removed and replaced by the witty punchlines you weren't quick enough to think of at the time, all you can really do is let them down. The person I am in real life, while connected to my on-stage persona, remains basically my act with hours and hours of sighing, tutting and genuine anger at inconsequential events put in between the jokes.

This is the person awaiting Gemma, beautiful and giggly Gemma. Why can't our potential last for ever? Now things will come to a head, one way or another, and the perfect anticipation will die. The odds of our succeeding together in the world are stacked so heavily against us. Faint heart ne'er won fair maiden, but it never lost her for good either. The nerves I get before a gig are nothing compared to the nerves I get before meeting someone I like, as so much more is at stake. I can always get another job if I need to, as the criteria I look for in employment are much more straightforward than in love. Real life is so much more scary than the dream.

I am now not only divided between Public Jon and Private Johnny but between my new contractual obligations and my old dreams of everlasting happiness. Earning money from my compulsions and perfectionism make even me question whether or not I have somehow subconsciously and not a little cynically cultivated such a persona from the beginning. Would I really have been so stupid as to spend eight years in misery for this moment of brief professional success? Or has it been more than that? If I can work out when I started to feel like I do then I can decide once and for all whether or not this is a temporary affectation or a deeper problem that should preclude me from spending time with someone on a more intimate basis.

There is no way I can meet Gemma like this, but I know that if I cancel she will be disappointed. I can hardly tell her it's because I have to write a book instead but then nor can I explain that delving into my past has revealed that I was always destined to be disappointed with the world and I don't feel as though it would be fair to drag her down with me. When my life flashes before my eyes, my aim is to make sure there are no scenes to rival those in horror films where the girl enters the room knowing that something is in there. I don't want to be screaming at myself not to go in when I know it was a mistake. People say you only live to regret the things you didn't do, not the things you did, but I disagree.

At some point I will explain everything to her and she will understand that in becoming another one of my 'Near Mrs' she has had a considerable escape, but for now I just need to tell her. I pull my phone from my pocket but it is switched off. I haven't had it on since my meeting, or was it already off before that? When it flashes and buzzes into life I see that I have a voicemail message, and listening to it I hear a voice I only faintly recognise.

'So, your name is Jon, is it? I just want you to know I've got your number you stupid fuck, and if you pull any more shit like that last text message I'll get this number traced and find you and come and break your fucking legs.'

Ah, yes. The Terminator. Charming man. I must admit when I realised he had got my name from my answerphone message my stomach dropped a yard or two – that was careless. He can't really do anything, probably won't do anything. Time to start typing – do it fast before you can change your mind.

> Gemma. I'm so sorry to do this to you, but I don't think I can make dinner tonight. I will explain everything soon, but for now please know just one thing: It's not you, it's me. x

Oh.

All I can do now is plan for tomorrow. Wiping my face on a towel, I come out of the bathroom and then, sitting down at my desk I begin another list, taking not just one day at a time, but breaking each day down into its requisite tasks. By compartmentalising life as I do I can tell myself that by executing each task perfectly I am living a perfect life. The problem is that sometimes when you put your head down and focus intently on each tiny step, making sure not to fall or step in anything unpleasant, by the time you eventually think to look up you realise that you have been walking for miles in completely the wrong direction. Could I find contentment in a kind of perfect misery?

In the end I know that I am married to my solitude, but I am oddly relieved by the thought of not having to look after Gemma, or anyone else for that matter, and that I will never again be able to let her down. This cowardice is simply how it is for me, the life I have chosen. I am not a pathetic figure, not lusting after love unrequited, but travelling alone, with my eye on the milometer – 60,000 miles coming soon to a dashboard near you.

An early start tomorrow – I have a book to write after all.

But before I can finish my list, the thought occurs to me:

Did you lock the door behind you when you came in?

TUESDAY

EPILOGUE

06.58

WAKE UP

It is only imperfection that complains of what is imperfect. The more perfect we are the more gentle and quiet we become towards the defects of others.
                                                        Joseph Addison

I complain because it is easier, I hate because it is easier. As a stand-up comedian I am used to receiving abuse. I can accept blind hatred because by definition it is so irrational. Like a child who says they hate something they haven't tasted, it is a response, a desire to be noticed more than anything. I hate things and I do so because it is clean and easy and makes me feel better about myself without having to ask why I don't get my own house in order first.

Had I been a TV executive in the 1980s there might well have been a light-entertainment show entitled *Jim Says 'Fix It Your Fucking Self!'* But that is my past, not my future.

I don't speak or write much about my happiest moments because for one thing they are very personal to me, but they don't strike me mostly because my memory of them is somewhat hazy. This is not because they were not important to me or because I was always blind drunk during them (though for some of them I almost certainly was) but simply because I didn't stop at any point to take mental notes of colour and texture for recounting at a later date. Happiness, like sleep, in order to be fully effective must involve some sort of yielding of conscious thought, in my opinion.

I realise that I have only one memory from my early childhood of even being aware of perfectionism, though I wouldn't have been able to describe it in anything like such grandiose terms, being as I was only about three or four years old.

The incident took place on an almost black and white afternoon, walking into town with my mum. I don't know whether the skies were genuinely so dark or whether, over time, all the colours have been bleached by my memory and all that remains are the people and the events. One day they will become blurred too, I suppose, and I won't remember whether or not this happened in life or in a dream. Lancaster town centre was just about the biggest thing I could imagine and that was a thrilling thought indeed. None of the fear of big cities like London existed then.

Though my memory of the day is black and white, two objects seem as vividly colourful to me now as they were on that particular day: my brand new Thomas the Tank Engine Wellington boots. From the moment I saw them in the bucket outside the shoe shop to the moment my mum relented and parted with what little money she had in those days, or three pounds of it at any rate, I have never wanted anything as much in my entire life. Nor has anything ever lived up to my expectation quite like those wellies in the days since.

'Do they fit you properly?' asked my mum as I ran frantically around the shop making choo-choo noises, wearing one Wellington boot and one trainer.

'Yes, yes, yes! Please buy them, Mummy. Pleeease!'

I could see what she meant by that question – she was looking for excuses to hate my new shoes and not buy them! Luckily I managed to see through that little scheme. These boots were what I wanted and I wasn't going to let a little thing like whether or not they warped and cut my young feet beyond recognition stand in the way of owning them.

For adults, most things lose their appeal once you own them, almost as if you have lost respect for them for even being attainable. People fall prey to this problem as well as meaningless objects like money, and

most of the attraction we feel for those eyes we meet 'across a crowded bar' (insert dry retching here) lies in the belief that they might simply be out of your range.

'Will you go out with me? WHAT? You will! Oh my God, that's absolutely … Hang on! Why? What's wrong with you?'

Questions rise to the surface and refuse to be answered by any but the most obvious and disappointing answers. Why do you like me? What's wrong with you? What's your ulterior motive? You are attractive, funny, intelligent … and what else? The nicer the person, the greater my distrust for their interest in me. The goals you set for yourself also lose their lustre as you achieve them.

'Well, if I did it then it can't be that hard, because I'm only me.'

This is how I sometimes feel about being a comedian – it was what I dreamed of in my teenage years and there are occasionally times when I feel almost embarrassed to have wasted my time dreaming of something that proved to be attainable, that being the opposite of what a dream should be. I sometimes wonder if I have lost respect for comedy because it didn't call me out. It didn't expect more than I could offer it. But then there are other times (fortunately more than I'm prepared to admit) when I love what I do and when I realise how

very lucky I am to be doing it. There are times when I feel so privileged I could scream in frustration at the fact that I can't share a little of it with everyone or all of it with someone.

If the experience in the shop was enough to try a parent's patience, the following half an hour must have been incredibly difficult on my mum, tugging gently at a toddler who could barely walk at the best of times, let alone now, as he insisted on stopping after each tiny step to stare triumphantly down at his feet. Still, despite all my stalling I don't remember her making me rush. Not then, or ever, in fact. She was happy to enjoy the look of sheer fascination set like stone across my face.

There were no puddles to splash in, but I wouldn't have dared jump into one anyway, for fear that it would make the boots dirty. The boots were perfect and so, while I was wearing them, was I. Adults pollute their world with a spectrum of unnecessary colours like taupe, salmon and azure, but children know of only four or five. These boots were proper, unadulterated blue, no messing around. There was no problem with the colour, or the shape or the shine on their toes, but something was wrong. It wasn't me, it wasn't my mum and it certainly wasn't the boots. It slowly dawned on me that it was simply *everything* else.

The reason I was stopping after each pace was that each new patch of ground revealed there was

something else to hate about the world that existed beyond my magical feet. The pavements I saw in my cartoons and in my head were perfectly smooth strips of Plasticine grey that not only could you 'eat your dinner off', but you could safely crawl on your hands and knees sucking up the sapphire-blue puddles that were spaced regularly along their length. This other world, this so-called *real* world, was nothing like that, now that I saw it for the first time up close, lurking beyond my wellies.

There were cracks in it. Literal cracks on the surface of my world!

There were dirty, brown, decaying leaf skeletons, piles of dog dirt, patches of bubble gum, uneven bumpy bits where holes had been filled with mismatching colours of concrete, there were frothing puddles of human spit and bum bombs from the birds. There were rusty old grids with frenzied patterns and illegible words written across them. The real world suddenly seemed such a horrible place when contrasted with my shiny blue shoes. If they were perfect then why couldn't everything else be perfect too?

I started to get worried that the pavement was going to ruin my shoes and that if I stood on a crack then the blue colour would seep out of them and down into the bowels of the earth in front of my very eyes and they would turn as grey as the sky and the surface would blister and crack. When I tried to avoid the cracks there were too many, and I noticed that my mother was walking right over them and I got worried that they were going to get her too! I started to cry because I thought it was all going to break and there was nothing I could do to help it. As my mother picked me up and took me into her arms I carried on crying because the sky wasn't blue and the clouds weren't chunky white blobs of angel delight and there were too many noises in the street that were hurting my head. Being in her arms made it better though, I remember that.

'Is it the boots?' she asked me.

'Yes, Mummy,' I sobbed. 'Can you take them off me please?'

I often wonder now, if I see a toddler crying helplessly at the feet of exasperated parents who keep asking for an explanation of what is wrong, if that child is going through what I went through that day. I wonder if they are learning the truth behind the lies they are shown to get them to go to sleep at night, the real world where animals don't talk but bite, where rain is cold and wet and dirty and where nothing is as colourful as a dream. They can't put it into words, just as I couldn't either, but the fear is real enough.

'What's wrong, honey? What is it?'

'It's everything, Daddy. Why is everything not like you promised it would be? Why?'

Years later, when I asked my mother if she remembered my boots and what happened to them, she explained that we had taken them back to the shop that very afternoon because she had thought they were hurting my feet. She told me she couldn't believe that I had wanted them so much and yet when they were gone I never once asked about them or wanted another pair. It doesn't surprise me. Those boots held up a mirror to an imperfect world and the reflection terrified me.

This story aside, I distrust those who have vivid recollections of all the events of their childhoods and significant moments after that because I think either that they are made up (not lies completely but re-imaginings of times and places constructed after the event) or else they cannot have been truly happy memories as some part of the brain was actively planning for a moment in the future when what was going on would need to be recalled, taking evidence almost. I cannot help but cringe looking upon people at a live event, who instead of enjoying the moment and seeing it for what it is, seem hell-bent on filming the whole thing through the crappy camera on the phone they hold high above their heads and point at the stage. Their memory will one day be built solely around the image on the screen and will reflect less and less the truth of what was really

happening at the time. Unhappy times seem to work in a different way altogether though, leaving behind mental scars whether you want them or not.

You can see that I can describe at length the face of a man who upset me on a train because I was making a conscious effort to remember him, perhaps so that I could gain revenge if ever I saw him again or perhaps, more generally, because I was trying to work out what was wrong with the situation I was in and how I could rectify it in future and prevent it from happening again. But could I describe in as much detail the face of the last woman I saw who made my heart leap out of my throat? Absolutely not. That moment, and the hundreds of others like them, electrified me so absolutely that I could barely tell you who *I* was when it happened, let alone where I was when it happened or which way the wind was blowing.

Something happens when you are overcome by positive emotion that forces your brain to surrender to it completely – perhaps this is 'the moment' I have argued against so vociferously earlier – and only someone truly cynical at heart would deny this feeling altogether. Almost always these emotions are triggered by other people. Is it possible to be so happy and feel such abandonment of sense alone? I don't think so, perhaps if only because being alone immediately demands an increased alertness on health and safety grounds.

Two people together on a beach can drink and doze and walk along hand in hand, knowing that should anything go wrong for one, the other would step in and take control. One person alone on the beach must always have one eye on not getting too drunk to find their way back to the hotel, not wandering too far from their possessions or getting sunburnt. In short, a part of the brain is always with the bags and wallets on the shore, even if the spirit is doing its best to float away in the warm, blue waters.

I am not saying that it is impossible to surrender to solitude altogether, only that there is an implied risk. I have read books about many men my age who have lusted after solitude and have gone to great lengths to find it – some moving even further away from society than Swindon, if you can imagine such a place! Everett Ruess (whose letters make up the amazing work *A Vagabond for Beauty*), Chris McCandless (whose exploits were written about in the book *Into the Wild*, later made into a Hollywood film) and perhaps the most famous of them all, Jack Kerouac, whose ramblings have come to define a generation, all lived their lives totally on their own terms and independently of their perceived duties in society.

As much as their stories enthral me, and inspire me to strengthen my resolve and accept my fate as someone more comfortable with his own company than in

large groups, I must concede that a fairly negative character trait links all three – a selfishness in pursuit of happiness entirely on their own terms. I have never been so determined to be on my own that I have forgotten my obligation as a son, as a brother and as a friend; I believe that those people who have stuck by me through my (at times) seemingly relentless efforts to quell any enjoyment of life deserve if nothing else my loyalty. My first thought on turning the last page of Keruoac's seminal *On the Road* was of how worried his mother must have been and how little time he seemed to have made to contact her during his travels.

Both Everett and Chris made the ultimate sacrifice in their searches for happiness, giving up their lives tragically young. Everett disappeared at the age of twenty and as inspired as I am by his love for nature and his determination to live a life outside of the 'rules and regulations' of normal practice, it still seems a tragic waste of an erudite and gifted writer and artist.

Humans are like balloons. Most outlive the joy they see and shrivel into obscurity, but some generate furious excitement and then, like Everett, simply drift skywards and are never seen again. To live and die on one's own terms is a basic human right, but sometimes I think we are all too close to our own feelings to be able to put them into context and perhaps, just

sometimes, we are not best placed to decide such things for ourselves.

As for what I can do to change myself? I don't know, but I am certain that I can. Writing this book has helped me put some issues to bed and I hope that it hasn't been a mistake writing so plainly the thoughts I have down on paper. If nothing else I suppose I might have amassed an army of people who think like I do, and supposing one of them is an architect, another a farmer, a doctor and so on, it is conceivable that we could construct a town for ourselves where there are only single tables in restaurants and all beds are constructed on top of existing furniture. New members would join all the time, I suspect, meaning that breeding would not be necessary; however, recreational intercourse could continue subject to approval by the town elders. If that town needs a clown then I will, of course, submit my application in writing.

Or perhaps not! I know that no matter how many times I fail, or how isolated I feel, I will never be able to stop looking for someone with whom I can share my life. However much I talk about how heavily the odds are stacked against success in love, like entering the national lottery, people do so because the prize is sufficient to justify the hope. I once saw an elderly couple dancing together in a ballroom in south Wales (don't ask how I came to be there), their interlocked bodies swaying gently with the music of their shared youth. Hands clasped together on one side, the other caressing her left hip and his shoulder, I could see that coiled round the lady's hand was a lead, at the bottom of which was a dog turning in a happy unison with its masters. For each of these three, everything they loved was spinning within a metre of their smiling faces and time, weather and the alphabetisation of their book cases were all an utter irrelevance.

If this moment of contented bliss is the prize at the end, then surely any amount of worry and stress incurred during the search is worthwhile? Here's to many more years on the hunt.

ACKNOWLEDGEMENTS

This book would not be what it is without the hard work of Natalie Jerome, Martin Noble and the team at HarperCollins.

I would not be the comic I am without the devotion and faith of Danny Julian, Addison Cresswell, Joe Norris and all at Off the Kerb.

Most notably, I wouldn't have a life worth living or writing about without the love of all my family, especially my mum, Elaine, and my sister, Tamsin, who bear the brunt of my moods.

I also owe huge thanks to all the audiences whose laughter has added fuel to my fire.